SIMPLE PRINCIPLES YIELD POWERFUL RESULTS

Of course you want good results—in doing your job, in reaching your goals, in maintaining good health, and in living your life. Here is good news for you: good results can be yours right now! How? Over years of observing people who have attained success, I long ago came to the conclusion, based on factual knowledge, that positive thinkers get positive and powerful results.

So certain am I that there is a definite relationship between positive thinking and positive results that I think an invariable scientific formula is involved. Explicitly stated it is this: think positively, image positively, pray positively, and believe positively, and powerful results will be yours. Helping you learn how to achieve powerful results, according to this formula, is the purpose of my book.

Norman Vincent Peale

Fawcett Crest Books
by Norman Vincent Peale:

THE AMAZING RESULTS OF POSITIVE THINKING

ENTHUSIASM MAKES THE DIFFERENCE

FAITH IS THE ANSWER

A GUIDE TO CONFIDENT LIVING

HAVE A GREAT DAY

INSPIRING MESSAGES FOR DAILY LIVING

THE NEW ART OF LIVING

POSITIVE IMAGING

THE POSITIVE PRINCIPLE TODAY

THE POWER OF POSITIVE THINKING

POWER OF THE PLUS FACTOR

SIN, SEX AND SELF-CONTROL

STAY ALIVE ALL YOUR LIFE

THE TOUGH-MINDED OPTIMIST

TREASURY OF JOY AND ENTHUSIASM

THE TRUE JOY OF POSITIVE LIVING

WHY SOME POSITIVE THINKERS GET POWERFUL
   RESULTS

WHY SOME POSITIVE THINKERS GET POWERFUL RESULTS

Norman Vincent Peale

FAWCETT CREST • NEW YORK

To

MYRON L. BOARDMAN,
*longtime friend
and associate,
with appreciation
and affection*

Contents

To The Reader

OF COURSE you want good results—in doing your job, in reaching your goals, in maintaining good health, and in living your life in general. Here is good news for you: good results can be yours. How? Over years of observing people who attained successful living, I long ago came to the conclusion, based on factual knowledge, that positive thinkers inevitably get positive and powerful results.

So certain am I that there is a definite relationship between positive thinking and positive or good results that I think an invariable scientific formula is involved. Explicitly stated it is this: think positively, act positively, image positively, pray positively, and believe positively, and powerful results will be yours. Helping you learn how to achieve powerful results, according to this formula, is the purpose of this book.

I hope you will stay with me in a reader-author team by reading this book from beginning to end. I

1

have explored practical, workable methods of positive thinking that will greatly enhance your life. By long study and experience I have discovered some simple principles that have worked for me and many others, when they are applied. It is also my pleasure to outline some of the amazing things I have personally found about the power of positive thinking, which I first wrote about many years ago in *The Power of Positive Thinking* and expanded later in other books. So let us proceed to the consideration of an exciting question—the answers to which can improve anyone's life—why some positive thinkers get powerful results.

I wish to express great appreciation to the two dedicated persons who helped immeasurably with this manuscript. One is my secretary, Sybil Light, who meticulously prepared it, and the other, my wife Ruth, who expertly edited it.

Norman Vincent Peale

1.

I've Got It Made

I'M GLAD that I have never been able to say or even
to think that I've got it made. I'm still dreaming,
still planning, still trying, still working, and everything is continuously exciting.

We hear people say, "At last I've got it made."
About achievers we admiringly exclaim, "He has
made it to the top. He's got it made." Or "She has hit
the jackpot. That woman sure has everything." So
it goes!

But I have sometimes noted something sad about
"got-it-maders"; a certain quality seems to have
gone out of them. The incentive, the drive, the
motivation that took them to the top has declined.
The old thrill and excitement of achievement aren't
like they once were. Now that these people have got
it made, the challenge has dimmed, and maybe the
enjoyment of getting there doesn't live up to expec-
tations. As one top achiever complained, "There

isn't much fun in life anymore. No challenges or problems like there were."

The president and chief executive officer of one of the most famous corporations in America had a spectacular rise in business. At thirty-five he was top man in a highly competitive industry. He had it made, or so it seemed. At forty he was tiring of it all, and at forty-five he'd "had it," to quote his downbeat evaluation of his career. "From now on," he complained, "I've just got to hold my own, keep some fellow from pushing me off my chair. It was a lot more interesting when I was fighting my way up the hard way. Those were the great days of my life. It isn't the same anymore."

But other men and women are geared differently. Having achieved one goal, they set another and repeat the old tried and true success pattern. They come up with fresh achievements. Having fulfilled old dreams, these people latch onto fresh dreams, bigger challenges, more exciting objectives. Thus it is that they have a perpetual delight in living and working and winning. Their enthusiasm never runs down. Theirs is a constantly renewing and exciting experience. Always they are zestful, eager, creative. They never have it made; they are always striving to make it.

The true flavor, the real fun, the continuous excitement is in the process of making it rather than in having made it. Happiness actually is found in striving for a goal rather than in settling down to enjoy the attained objective. It is found in setting another goal and enthusiastically going for that goal in the same old competitive, innovative spirit.

Happiness at last comes to those who never lose the excitement of going after new goals, who are forever wanting to achieve something better. If you are a winner in a big way or even in a moderate way, you may conclude that since you have it made, you may rest upon your laurels. Be careful, for the result of doing that can be no more laurels. Perhaps more important, there may be no more of the joy of striving.

One of the most genuinely happy men I ever knew was the late Amos Parrish, perhaps the top sales idea expert in the department store industry. Though he stuttered all his life, store executives would come annually to A. P.'s lectures, packing the grand ballroom of a big New York City hotel to listen to him talk about marketing. This was an outstanding and remarkable achievement, but it was only one of his goal realizations. Even as he grew older, his mind was alert, constantly delivering amazing new ideas. When I would compliment him on some big success, he would brush it aside. "Listen to this idea I'm working on now. This is a h-h-honey," he would excitedly stutter.

When word came that he was dying at ninety-four years of age, I telephoned him. I always loved him and owed him much because he had always inspired me. "Hey there," he said with his usual enthusiasm, "I've got a new idea. This one is a beaut." And he went on to outline an exciting new goal. There was, of course, no talk of dying, only talk about the excitement of living. But two days later he was dead of a progressive disease. A. P. never really had it made, though he was a very successful businessman. He was always involved in the further making of it and having the time of his life in the process.

This unique, unforgettable man brings to mind another equally remarkable friend, the famous baseball executive Branch Rickey. He was successively head of the Saint Louis Cardinals, the former Brooklyn Dodgers, and the Pittsburgh Pirates His book, *The American Diamond,* is a classic on the game of baseball. At a dinner celebrating Branch Rickey's fifty years in baseball, a reporter asked him, "What was your greatest experience in your half-century in this great American sport?" Pulling down his beetling eyebrows, Rickey snapped, "Don't know. I haven't had it yet." Despite his many distinguished achievements, this man would never assume he had it made. To him it was always still in the making. As a result, his career went from one higher level to another, there being no halting of his achievements.

I was the speaker on a recent Sunday morning in the Crystal Cathedral in Garden Grove, California. This amazing structure was crowded to overflowing by a congregation, according to the newspapers, numbering eleven thousand people in two services and filling every auditorium on the campus. Surrounded by landscaped grounds where sparkling fountains toss their spray, this huge steel and glass church is the spiritual home of millions who receive its message weekly by television.

My presence was occasioned by the observance of the thirtieth anniversary of Dr. Robert Schuller, the minister who, beginning with five hundred dollars and a lot of faith, built this great church. On this special Sunday Dr. Schuller announced plans for another center to serve family needs. One might have thought that he too had it made, but for a unique group of positive people there are always new goals to be built on old goals already achieved.

Regardless of all you may have done to realize your goals, you can do still more; to all your previously achieved goals, you can add other exciting objectives. I want to remind you, if you need reminding, that your future stretches out before you, packed with all kinds of marvelous opportunities. You haven't made it yet, no matter how outstanding your achievements have been. The best, your best, is yet to be. Never look at the great things you have done and say, "Not bad, not bad at all. I've got it made." Instead tell yourself that the splendid things you have accomplished are just indications of what you can do. Believe, always believe, and never doubt that your future lies entrancingly out there ahead of you. Then you will proceed from one level of achievement to another in a life pattern of continuous growth and development.

Basic to our American way of life is the doctrine that any person, under the free opportunities afforded by democracy, can rise to the level of his belief and talent. The quality of one's belief and thinking has been demonstrated to be superior in importance to talent. In fact, thought and faith have often released talent previously unsuspected. Realizing the importance of these features, I have successfully persuaded many people that by positive thinking and by faith in God and in themselves, they can release extraordinary ability from their personalities. By this method many supposedly ordinary persons have become quite extraordinary individuals. But quite beyond anything I or other writers in the field of inspiration and motivation may have done, the climate of America has of itself produced amazing life stories.

In a midwestern city my wife, Ruth, and I were guests in the exquisitely beautiful home of an unusually successful businessman, one who has created an innovative and famous enterprise. Previously I had the privilege of conferring upon him the prestigious Horatio Alger Award given to distinguished Americans who have risen from poverty to positions of honor and influence.

"Where were you born, Dave?" I asked our host.

"I don't know. I think Atlantic City" was his surprising reply. "Nor do I know who my parents were. I was an orphan and grew up with foster parents. I was sent out into the world with only a few dollars in my pocket." After many vicissitudes, this orphan boy got a busboy job with a restaurant owner in Fort Wayne, Indiana.

A hard worker who had the ability to think, Dave did a good job. Eventually his boss sent him to see what could be done with a small restaurant in

Columbus, Ohio, which was failing. But Dave had no success with this restaurant until he realized that he had too many items on the menu which required a large inventory that made it difficult to make a profit. With a limited menu, he turned the restaurant around. He took his profits and opened a hamburger restaurant, because he had loved hamburgers since he was a child. He named his little restaurant after one of his daughters, Wendy, and it gradually took off. Dave Thomas always used the best beef, constantly added new features, and created attractive outlets. He used his good mind and his strong faith to such advantage that currently the Wendy's chain consists of some 3,200 restaurants and is rated at the top of this type of food business.

If you were to ask Dave Thomas if he has it made, meaning that the possibilities for his development have been reached, you would receive a strong negative reply. Men of his stature are the type of persons who constantly improve the American economy. They are perpetual new goal setters who proceed from one level to ever-higher levels of achievement.

It so happens that I am in what may be called the speaking business. That is to say, I accept many engagements to address state and national business conventions, community gatherings, and other functions. Long ago I discovered that this business is one in which you never have it made. No matter how long you have been speaking or how well you may have done it, the engagement tonight is the one that matters. You must do this one to the very best of your ability. Whatever reputation you may have may predispose the audience in your favor before you begin tonight's talk, but that lasts only a few minutes. You will be judged by *this* crowd on what you do *this* night.

At a national business convention meeting at which I was scheduled to speak, I was talking before the session with a young, aspiring speaker. "How long have you been at this speaking business?" he asked.

"About fifty years," I replied.

"Boy, you are fortunate. You have it made. And I'm going to have it made myself pretty soon."

"I am sorry to disabuse you," I said, "but I do not have it made. I must give this speech as if I had never spoken before, and I must give all that I'm capable of to this audience."

Several years later I was on a program with this same speaker, now older and wiser. "I know what you meant back there that night in Chicago. Now just when I think at last I've got it made, I get slapped down in a speech and feel like a beginner all over again."

"You and me both," I replied ruefully as we shared a moment of camaraderie.

On the basis of this philosophy of the "I've got it made" concept, what is the most successful principle of goal setting and goal achieving? As a starter let me set forth some rules that I have known to be effective, and then I will develop them further as I go along.

1. Think about where you want to get in life.
2. Come to a firm decision about your basic objective.
3. Formulate and write your goal in a sharp, clear statement, and eliminate all fuzziness of thought.
4. Study and learn all that you can about your goal and how to get there.
5. Fix a time for achieving your goal.
6. Pray about your decision to be sure that it is right. If it is not right, it is wrong, and nothing wrong turns out right.
7. Give your goal complete and unremitting effort, and never give up trying.
8. Apply positive thinking.
9. Never assume you have it made. One goal attained leads to another and on and on.

One technique I developed for myself is to write a goal on a card and keep it in my shirt pocket over my heart, the traditional seat of emotional response. My goal, I decided upon in my youth, is to help as many people as possible to live at their highest potential by persuading them to become believers, positive thinkers, people of faith. Many years ago I wrote this goal on a card and have carried it in my shirt pocket ever since. I have had other goals from time to time and have written each of them on cards so that now and then my pocket has been filled with written goals. As I achieved them, I removed the cards. Sometimes I have also copied goals set by other people and carried them in my pocket and prayed about them for friends who also used the shirt pocket technique.

I have often described this method of goal attainment in speeches before sales and business conventions, and many people have used it effectively. For example, a young man attended a national insurance convention where I outlined the shirt-pocket technique in a speech. He was a dedicated agent, but he wasn't doing too well. My speech convinced him that the principal reason for his lack of success was that he really did not expect to set any records. He determined to take a more positive attitude, to visualize himself as achieving better results.

This convention was held early in the new year. Following the speech, he went to his room in the hotel and had a "good ruthless think session," as he described it to me later. Then and there he set a sales goal for the year at a figure that "left him breathless" since it was far beyond anything he had ever done. Here is what he wrote on the card that he carried in his shirt pocket all year long. That it contributed to his success he has no doubt.

> I image this new year as my best year.
> I affirm enthusiasm, energy,
>   and pleasure in my work.
> As a positive thinker, I believe I will
>   do 10 percent better than last year.
> God will help me reach this goal.

"At the end of that year what result did you have?" I asked.

"Believe it or not," he replied, "I hit that 10 percent increase smack on the nose. Had I not used your shirt-pocket technique I would still be fumbling along near the bottom of our agency. I firmly believe it gave me a new, positive attitude that brought out a talent I didn't know I had. Anyway, I'm moving up now."

"When you went for that 10 percent increase, a figure that is really amazing, how did you feel?"

"Well, you know," he said, "it's funny, but I just knew I could do it. I'm a committed Christian, and every day I said, 'I can do all things through Christ who strengthens me' (Phil. 4:13), or 'If you have faith as a mustard seed, . . . nothing will be impossible for you' (Matt. 17:20)." He added, "Those Bible promises really work. I know that for sure, because they are working for me."

"You've got it made?" I said admiringly with a question mark in my tone.

"Oh, no, I haven't. I'm just starting on my way, and I've got an awful lot to learn. The old failure pattern is still in me and could grab control if I let down. But I'm not going to be lulled into a false sense of security by saying, 'I've got it made.' "

Smart fellow! He was turning his insecurity into a creative motivation.

Turn back to that list of nine rules for reaching a goal, and note the emphasis on knowing definitely where you want to go and the importance of setting a time for reaching your objective. This sort of clear, definite focusing of aim I consider to be very important. If you know exactly where you wish to go and when you expect to get there, you are mentally summoning all the immense force of your personality into action, and you are directing that force to the support of your objectives.

I wish to repeat here an incident I have often used to demonstrate the power inherent in this principle. Playing golf one day, I sliced a ball into the rough at the fairway's edge. A young fellow raking leaves there politely helped me find my ball. "Sometime, Dr. Peale, I would like to talk to you about myself," he said rather hesitatingly.

"When?" I asked.

Startled he said, "Oh, I don't mean now. Just sometime."

"Sometime seldom comes," I said. "Meet me at the eighteenth hole in about thirty minutes and we will talk." Later sitting in the shade of a tree, I asked the young fellow's name and said, "Now, what's on your mind?"

"Oh, I don't know. I just want to get somewhere."

"Where?" I asked. "Exactly where do you want to get?"

He looked bewildered. "Oh, I don't know where. I just know I want to get somewhere else from where I am now. I don't know just where."

"And when do you plan to get where you don't know where you want to get?"

Confused by these questions and perhaps even a bit irritated, he grumbled, "How do I know when? Just sometime. I want to get somewhere sometime."

Then I asked him what he could do best, and he replied that he did nothing very well and he didn't know what he could do the best. To my question about what he liked to do, he thought awhile and then answered that he didn't know what he particularly liked to do.

"Well, now, here's your situation as I see it: you want to get somewhere, but you don't know where. And you do not know when you expect to get there. Besides that, you don't know what you can do the best nor what you like to do. Is that about it?"

He glumly nodded his head, "Guess I'm a total flop."

"Not at all. You are just not organized or focused. You've got a nice personality, a good head on your shoulders, and a desire for improvement, and that desire is trying to motivate you. I like you and believe in you."

I suggested that he spend two weeks thinking about his future, that he decide definitely upon a goal, and that he write that goal, using the fewest possible words. Then he was to compute when he might reasonably expect to reach his goal. I asked him to write these decisions on a card and come back to tell me about it.

Promptly two weeks later he showed up quite a different fellow, at least in spirit. He was focused and better organized. He knew what he wanted: to be the plant manager of the company where he was working. He explained that the present incumbent was due to retire in five years, and his goal was to be offered that position at that time. He developed such know-how and leadership ability during that five-year period that when the job finally opened, he had no competition for it.

I might add that now, some years later, he is still

in the same position and is indispensable to his employers. He achieved the goal he decided upon following that golf course conference. He is happy and satisfied.

A combination of goal setting, positive thinking, visualizing and believing leads to a successful outcome in most of the problems with which each of us must deal. If you want to have it made, whatever the situation, I suggest putting these four creative factors into active practice.

Take the vital matter of life correction, when seemingly so many things need a turnaround—attitude, health, personality. Sometimes life may break down at many points under differing pressures. Instead of having it made, everything seems to be unmade, sometimes all at once.

A perfect example of this is the man I met on a speaking engagement in a Canadian city. Seldom have I encountered a more dynamic, positive, and obviously happy man. He presided over the meeting of some two thousand persons, and I was terribly impressed by his spirit and attitude. Finally, out of curiosity, I said, "You are terrific. Tell me, how did you get this way?"

"It's a long story," he said, "but I'll shorten it to spare you. Everything in my life seemed to break up all at once. It all went sour. And later I learned it was because I, as a person, had broken up. I went sour. My concerned wife tried everything to build me up and to improve the distressing circumstances. Finally she remembered your book, *The Power of Positive Thinking,* and asked me to read it. The

title sort of struck me, but when I found it had
religion in it, I chucked it, for I was off religion,
preachers, and the church. But goaded by my wife,
to whom I am devoted, I stuck with the book, decid-
ing I would bypass the religious stuff and read only
the commonsense parts. But I ended up by taking it
all, including the religious part, hook, line, and
sinker."

His wife, who was listening to her husband's recital, said, "Just look at that wonderful guy. Everything broke up for him, but through your book God
put it all back together again."

"Yes," he said, "but I worked out an idea better
than anything in your book. And just to show you
how I appreciate what you did for me, I will let you
use this terrific idea in your next book."

So here it is: "One day," he said, "the thought
came to me that with God's help, I was greater than
anything that could happen to me. This resulted in
an affirmation I use every day. I pull myself up to
full height and say: 'I deny the power of the adverse.' Note I didn't say I deny the adverse but the
power of the adverse."

"You have come about as near as anyone I know
to having it made," I said, "because you have obviously become the master of your circumstances."

"Want to know when I became master?" he replied. "Well, I'll tell you. It was in the religious part
of your book which, like a dope, I wanted to bypass.
I'm certainly no saint, but I am now a believer. To
that extent I do believe I am on the way to having
it made, though I still have a long way to go."

Let's return to those four basic factors I referred to earlier that are involved in successful outcomes: goal setting, positive thinking, visualizing, and believing. With that combination, almost any adverse situation can be worked out for the best. One big problem relates to health. Judging from the mail we receive in our office, which runs into the thousands, I'd say health is problem number one. Money or job problems rank second, marital problems third. Overcoming a health problem and enjoying physical well-being are the top blessings of this life. Good health is profoundly precious.

Having it made in health is a top achievement, one that is desired by everyone. A combination of overindulgence in alcohol and in food, incessant smoking, and high tension had undermined the once rugged health of a friend I will call Joe (he said I may use his story if I don't use his real name). Joe had become obese and developed high blood pressure. He puffed up stairways, red in the face. His doctor finally let him have it straight—Joe could recover his health if he got on top of the drinking, smoking, eating, and tension. "But," the doctor concluded, "I don't know whether you have what it takes to reconstruct a healthy lifestyle."

This doctor knew that his last remark would anger Joe because he is one of those he-men who think they can do just about anything. So he reacted by bringing the drinking, smoking, and tension under pretty good control, but the eating problem proved his waterloo. He just couldn't push back from the table. He went on diet after diet, but none of them worked. The reason was simple: he didn't really work at any of them. He had to compensate for giving up the liquor and cigarettes, didn't he? So he rationalized his excessive food intake.

The doctor said, "Positive thinking and spiritual treatment are what you need. And, Joe, you've got to take off at least forty pounds. If you do that, added to what you have already done, I'm sure your blood pressure will go right down."

I might explain that the doctor and Joe and I are mutual friends, which is perhaps why the doctor sent Joe to me. When Joe came to see me, he had a negative outlook.

"I just can't change my eating habits. There is no way I can shed forty pounds," Joe complained to me.

"Oh, yes, you can. I know you can. I was told I had to take off thirty-five pounds, and I felt like you, that I couldn't do it. But I changed my mental attitude and took a positive approach. The pounds rolled off, the blood pressure went down, and I have never been healthier, just like you are going to be. So are you ready to start?"

"What choice have I got with Doc and you ganged up against me?" Joe grumbled.

"Not against you, *for* you," I said.

"Now, Joe, here is what I am going to help you do. Set a weight goal, practice positive thinking, visualize the results, and have lots of faith." We subtracted 40 from his weight of 200 to get the goal of a healthy 160.

"Why, I haven't weighed that since college."

"So what?" I said. "We're going back to stream-lined youth." He made a face.

Next we added the timing. When was he to achieve the goal? We set a date nine months away. Then we developed a new image of him as a slim 160. He was to think of himself with that midsection bulge gone, clothes hanging beautifully loose on his newly slender six feet one inch frame. And best of all, no guilt feeling for overeating was part of that image.

The last thing we discussed was his need to re-read *The Power of Positive Thinking*. He groaned at this one, but I said, "You've got to believe, to know that you can do this. And you will need a big dose of faith to emerge and remain exactly what the insurance table says you should be, namely, 160 pounds. Visualize that blood pressure as normal. Every day affirm, 'With God's help my blood pressure is going down, down, down, as the pounds roll off, off, off.'"

Joe got into the spirit of this slenderizing process. He became enthusiastic about physical renewal. Without his realizing it, he began to have a mental and spiritual renewal as well. He reached his goal in the time set. He felt better than he had in years. He went around telling everyone he had the blood pressure of a twenty-one year old.

"I've got it made weight-wise," he said one day when we were eating a lunch of clear soup, cottage cheese, and gelatin together. "I've got it made . . . thanks to Doc and you and," he added to my sur-prise, "the blessed Lord Jesus." He flushed a bit self-consciously at this last remark, because he was never one to talk religiously. But a bit belligerently, he said, "I've been praying all the way to 160 pounds."

So name your goal, and apply the positive principles. The day will come when you can thankfully say, "I've got it made." Then go for still another goal. You will be helped toward your goals by reading the next chapter, "Belief Power Gets Powerful Results."

2.

Belief Power Gets Powerful Results

"BORN TO LOSE." That ultranegative statement caught my eye as I strolled through a crooked little street in Kowloon, Hong Kong. I stared at those words in the window of a tattoo shop. It appeared that this was one of the slogans a customer could have tattooed on his body. Flags, mermaids, and other of the usual tattoos were also offered.

Astounded, I entered the shop and said to the Chinese man, "Does anyone actually have 'Born to lose' tattooed into his flesh?"

"Yes, some." But then tapping his head, he added in broken English, "Before tattoo on chest, tattoo on mind."

Failure begins in your thoughts when you hold the idea that you are actually incapable, that you are born to lose. So to counteract failure, develop the ability to believe. Tell yourself in no uncertain terms, "I was born to be a winner." To be that, you will just have to be a believer because winners are always believers. Losers are never real believers.

What is a believer? A believer in what? The answer to both questions is a belief in God, in life, in the future, in your spouse, in your kids, in your job, in your country and, last but certainly not least, in yourself. A man objected once when he heard me say this. "I'm a believer in God all right; but as such I am humble and, therefore, not a self-believer."

"Well," I replied, "if you don't believe in yourself, you don't much believe in God. He made you." And I quoted a sign I saw in our drugstore in Pawling, New York, picturing an upstanding little boy: "I believe in me, for God made me and He don't make no junk."

A notable American scholar, one of our wisest men, was William James, a professor of philosophy, anatomy, and psychology. It might be said that he was professor of mind, body, and emotions. (He ranks perhaps with Emerson and Thoreau in his vast knowledge of personality and successful living.) Here is how William James rated belief: "Belief at the beginning of a doubtful undertaking is the one thing that will guarantee the success of any venture."

So what is the *one* thing that guarantees success? Not knowledge, not education, not training, not experience, not money. It is belief. Belief in a project and belief in yourself are vital to success. Naturally other qualifications are extremely important, but the primary factor, the one basic essential, is belief— the belief that *you can* generate the powerful results you want. Another name for belief is positive thinking. It is a fact that some positive thinkers get positive results. William James declared, "Be not afraid of life. Believe that life is worth living and your belief will help create that fact."

Believers are a terrific breed of men and women. Nothing daunts them. They are afraid of nothing. If they have doubts, they rise above them. They become persons of power. These big, rugged souls sweep everything before them. They are doers, achievers, winners. They have the magic word—*belief*.

It is my conviction, based on knowledge of such people over many years and in all kinds of circumstances, that believers can overcome or solve or successfully live with any problem they will ever have to face. Some problems can be extremely difficult, even horrendous. But they don't really appear that way to believers, because believers bring up against any problem the assurance that it can be handled.

The person of belief never goes crawling through life on his hands and knees, whining and whimpering that it's all too much, that he is being treated unfairly. Instead such a person looks adversity straight on and then affirms, "As a child of the good God, I am greater than anything that can happen to me."

I believe that you and I were made to be winners. We were created to be great, not little. To overcome weakness and become a great human being, be a believer. Remember those power-packed words, "If you have faith as a mustard seed, . . . *nothing* will be impossible for you" (Matt. 17:20; emphasis added).

Memory, at the most unexpected times and places, can turn up things, people, and events seemingly long forgotten. This miracle of remembrance happened to me not long ago. I was walking on Fifth Avenue at the corner of Thirty-fifth Street when this flashback happened. In an instant I was transported back to the autumn of 1933 and to Fred.

I had known Fred in Brooklyn a few years previously but had not seen him since then. Now here he was coming along the avenue with the same old squared shoulders and peaceful look on his face. It was an affectionate reunion. "How goes it with you?" I asked. This meeting, I must explain, was at the bottom of the Great Depression of the 1930s, perhaps the lowest period economically in American history. Factories were closed. Empty stores all over the city testified to business failures. People had been let go by the hundreds of thousands, wages and salaries had been cut not once but several times. Soup kitchens and bread lines served long queues of people, some of whom were once affluent. It was widely asserted that no one over thirty years old had the slightest chance of getting a job. Such was the situation when I met Fred on once-prosperous Fifth Avenue that October afternoon.

He was wearing a blue serge suit. When old and long-used, they had the characteristic of becoming very shiny. Fred's was especially evident of long wear. But when he spoke, it was in his same old cheerful tone. "Oh, I'm all right. Just fine. Don't you spend any time worrying about me. It's true that I've been out of work for quite a while, but every morning I come into the city and tramp the streets looking for a job. You see, I just know that somewhere in this big city is a job for me, and I'm going to keep on hunting for it. I'll find it."

"You're keeping that big smile of yours going," I commented admiringly.

"Well, that makes sense, doesn't it? You see, I read somewhere that it requires sixty-four facial muscles to frown and only fourteen to smile. So why overwork your face?" Then he outlined more of his philosophy. He believed that a deep desire for a job would in time be rewarded by a compensatory satisfaction of that desire. "I heard you quote the poet John Burroughs once who said something to the effect that 'mine own will come to me.' "

But the touching thing about Fred was his faith, his belief. "I was raised by believing parents. We had very little, but that never fazed Mother. She would always say, 'The Lord will provide.' And do you know something, He always did. He never failed Mother once," and he added after a pause, his lip twitching a bit, "He won't fail me either." Then standing on the great avenue amidst throngs of unemployed people looking for work, he quoted the old biblical words, "I have been young, and now am old; yet have I not seen the righteous forsaken, nor his seed begging bread" (Ps. 37:25 KJV). He looked rather defiantly at me. "And no matter how tough it may get, I believe that. Mother and Father—and you [punching me affectionately in the chest] taught me to be a believer. So I just go on hoping and believing and looking."

As he moved along the street, I stood watching him. The sunlight on that shiny old blue serge suit suggested for a moment a knight's armor, its wearer riding in search of the Holy Grail, his sword of the spirit flashing bright.

What happened? He got a job with a man who had some genius for inventing things. In this innovative climate, Fred, who had a fertile mind, had an idea that took off. After a lot of struggle, belt tightening, and belief, Fred and the other man became quite successful. He lived constructively, had a fine family, and was respected by all who knew him.

Some years ago a Sunday was observed in which laymen were invited to speak in the pulpits of New York churches. I asked Dale Carnegie, who was a special friend of mine, to take on this assignment. Dale, author of the American classic *How to Win Friends and Influence People*, probably taught more men and women to speak in public through his courses than any man in America. He gave an unforgettable talk that Sunday morning.

But at one point his voice faltered. He was so deeply moved that he had to stop talking for what seemed a long moment. A hush fell over the big congregation. He was speaking of his youth. He described the poverty in which his family lived; sometimes there was no food in the house. "But not even this daunted Mother's faith," said Dale. "She went about the little house singing the wonderful old hymn 'What a Friend We Have in Jesus.' Calmly she assured Father and all of us children that the

Lord will provide. And," he added, "I cannot recall ever going to bed hungry. Necessities came to us in strange and even miraculous ways through Mother's powerful belief."

As I listened to unforgettable Dale Carnegie that day, it occurred to me that poverty was a source of motivation to some of our greatest Americans. It made them determined to lift themselves and their families to a better economic level. A powerful belief, usually derived from their religious training, made them believe that they could do so. I learned from Fred on the street and Dale Carnegie in the pulpit that neither economic depression nor setback such as loss of a job can permanently hold the positive-thinking person down, because in him is the ability to rebound. The lower he falls, the higher he bounces back up. Luck does not do it, nor do fortuitous circumstances, nor does it just happen for some reason. It is the power of belief that makes the difference, a big robust difference.

What causes men and women to get good results even out of harsh situations is this tough, resilient, unshakable belief that pervades their thought patterns. They have what is variously called faith, belief, or conviction that with the help of the Greater Power, they can overcome every difficulty. They have a deep inner feeling that they have what it takes to overcome, and they do not allow self-defeating negative thoughts to overwhelm this positive certainty. So become a believer, no matter how firmly you may have to discipline yourself or how long and hard you may have to work at doing so. Your future depends upon it.

I knew a man who conducted personnel studies for companies. He was also a sales trainer and was particularly successful in developing the unused potential in people. Melvin Evans was responsible for shifting people from jobs in which they were not doing so well to others in which he thought their talents could be better used. He had good to spectacular results. He used to describe his function as the "remaking people business," and he was extraordinarily capable in this capacity. He genuinely liked people, believed in them, and could perceive and bring out their hitherto untapped capabilities.

One case was that of a young man doing a routine clerical job. Evans was impressed by his outgoing, pleasant manner. He worked efficiently and was always thinking up new methods to increase productivity. Besides all this, he motivated others working alongside him to approach their jobs with more enthusiasm. Evans became convinced that this young man, Jack, possessed capabilities not being used.

"How do you feel about this company?" Evans asked.

"Best in the world," responded Jack. "I get a big kick out of working here. I'm going for my CPA."

"Want to know what I think about you, Jack? It may surprise you, but I think you have the makings of a real salesman. You have such enthusiasm for this product that you could sell it effectively and set a top record, benefiting the company tremendously and yourself as well."

At this surprising evaluation, another side of Jack surfaced. It was fear and self-disbelief. "Oh, no, Mr. Evans. I feel comfortable in this job. I know the routine. It's like a second home to me. I'd be like a fish out of water, and I just know I would never make it in selling." This showed his negative self-appraisal and fear of leaving the sheltered nest.

But Evans was firm. "You don't know your own self, son. All you need to do is make a mental shift from a nonbeliever to a believer. You must get acquainted with your real self."

Finally Jack was persuaded to enter the sales training course. To his surprise, he found it interesting, and the instructor told Evans, "I think you've discovered a guy who could be a born salesman. But he still lacks self-confidence."

"That will come," replied Evans.

Finally the time came to go on the road, out among the customers, and Jack was really nervous. But Melvin Evans said, "I'm going with you, Jack. We'll work at least part of the territory together." He introduced the new salesman to some of the people with whom he would do business. They all liked Jack because he was so outgoing. Jack carefully watched Evans demonstrate the selling process. And he picked up something even more important in their time together. Evans let his faith and belief in himself come through, and he transferred this faith to Jack. Soon Jack came to actually believe in Jack. He began to get a new concept of himself and with it the feel of success. As a result, excitement began to take over in him.

Then one day Evans told the young salesman that he had to leave him. He laid out the rest of the sales trip for Jack to do on his own. "Just go on liking people. Be friendly and believe in your product and," he added, "in yourself."

"I'm sure going to feel mighty alone," muttered Jack.

"You're never alone," said Evans.

Jack's subsequent success verified Evan's judgment of the young man's potential. Persuading self-doubting people to believe in themselves, as Melvin Evans did with Jack, is one of the prime objectives of this book.

This belief factor is an amazing force of almost incredible power. It contains all the positives in concentrated form. I have been asked by some people who want to seem nonreligious, "Must you have religious faith to have belief?" My answer is, "It sure does help."

For example, a story that appeared in a Chattanooga, Tennessee, newspaper told of four women in a dress shop, three clerks and one customer. The latter was in a dressing room putting on her clothes after trying on several new dresses. All of a sudden the shop door burst open and in came a big tough-looking man, a knife in one hand and a revolver in the other. "Hand over your money," he ordered.

All the three women clerks could put together was fifty-five dollars. This enraged him. "Lie down on the floor, and if you make a move, I'll kill you."

Then he heard the woman in the dressing room. He pushed and manhandled her, taking her money. He threatened her and cut her slightly with his knife. Then the woman reacted. Pulling herself to full height, she said in a strong, authoritative voice to the marauder, "Stop this. In the name of Jesus Christ, I command you to leave us alone. Stop this wickedness!" A look of astonishment came over the thief's face. Bewildered, he turned and ran from the shop, leaped into a car where a woman accomplice was at the wheel, and sped away. Later he was captured by police, and when interrogated, he said, "That woman had a power like I've never seen before." When this amazing power is turned on, belief gets the most amazing results.

This incident reminds me of a conversation I had with a middle-aged waitress, an outgoing, positive woman, in a motel coffee shop one morning when I was on a speaking trip. Although it was raining hard that morning, she greeted me by informing me it was going to be a great day. Right then and there this charming person made my day. In the course of my meal I discovered that she had put two children through college and had two more coming along. "My faith helped me do it. You see, I'm a believer," she explained.

She stated that, as a young couple, she and her husband lived in poverty. "I came to hate poverty. It destroys the soul. We were on relief and that galled me. It ate at my self-respect. My dear husband was sinking lower into despair. It was then that I read Luke 9:1." She stood by my table in that coffee shop and recited those great words: "Then He called His twelve disciples together and gave them power and authority over all demons and to cure diseases."

She continued, "Now that said something to me. I am a disciple of the Lord, and I am given authority over demons. Poverty is a demon. It is bad, very bad. As a believer, I took that authority. Well, it's a long story and it sure wasn't easy, but with the good Lord's help, my husband and I killed that demon of poverty."

With something like awe I shook hands with this great human being, this great believer, and went away inspired. I considered my own demons; most of us have them. I decided right then and there that I too would take the authority given to us as believers. One thing that came out of that experience is this book in which I want to emphasize that you can be an overcomer through the great power of belief. Whatever the difficulty, you can rise victoriously above what now defeats you. Believe that because it is the truth, the great big wonderful, undeniable truth.

Some of you may very much want this kind of belief going for you, but things have been, perhaps still are, really rough. What do you do when you have had (or are having) an extra tough time or have made some bad mistakes? When this question comes up, I am likely to remember the day a young lawyer came to see me. He was in deep despair and completely hopeless. He had been let go, at least temporarily, by a big law firm for having made a serious mistake. I thought it rather unfair to so penalize a beginner for one mistake, even a big one. I recall reading some years ago that Mrs. Knox of Knox Gelatin had a sign posted in her plant: "He deserves to break his own neck who stumbles twice on the same stone." At least she would give employees a second chance.

At any rate this dejected young lawyer paced up and down, upbraiding himself. "How could I be so dumb, so stupid? Here is my career gone down the drain and at the very start," he moaned, then slumped in a chair, the picture of utter despondency. At the moment I happened to have on my desk a column written by the late Grove Patterson in the *Toledo* [Ohio] *Blade*, a classic article by the great newspaper editor. I read it to the young man, and its effect upon him was miraculous. This column made such a lasting impression on me when I first read it years ago that I incorporated it in my autobiography, *The True Joy of Positive Living*, and I reprint it here.

A boy, a long time ago, leaned against the railing of a bridge and watched the current of the river below. A log, a bit of driftwood, a chip floated past. Again the surface of the river was smooth. But always, as it had for a hundred, perhaps a thousand, perhaps a million years, the water slipped by, under the bridge. Sometimes the current went more swiftly, and again quite slowly. But always the river flowed on under the bridge.

Watching the river that day the boy made a

discovery. It was not the discovery of a material thing, something he might put his hand upon. He could not even see it. He had discovered an idea. Quite suddenly, yet quietly, he knew that everything in his life would someday pass under the bridge and be gone, like water. And the boy came to like those words "under the bridge." All his life thereafter the idea served him well and carried him through, although there were days and ways that were dark and not easy. Always when he had made a mistake that couldn't be helped, or lost something that could never come again, the boy, now a man, said, "It's water under the bridge." And he didn't worry unduly about the mistakes after that and he certainly didn't let them get him down—because it was "water under the bridge."

The young man listened intently as I read this piece to him. He sat quite still for long moments. Then he rose, gripped my hand, and said feelingly, "Okay, I get the message. I will draw what know-how I can from this experience and let it go like 'water under the bridge.'" He walked out of my office that day a renewed believer in himself, and he also had belief in his future which, incidentally, turned out to be a very good one.

The tendency of people to depreciate themselves is widespread. But seldom have I received a letter quite so depreciatory, such a consummate self put-down, as came to my desk recently. It is from a woman, and I quote it in part.

I know this letter will probably never reach you personally but I'll write it anyway. Dr. Peale I have this big problem about myself. I have no self-confidence. I feel stupid and so unworthy of God's love. I wonder why He keeps me around, sometimes I wonder why was I born? My husband has a company and he is so smart. The two of us, in my opinion, don't compare.

I'm a quitter! I came from a broken home. I feel insecure and unloved. I guess that's why it's hard for me to believe that God really loves me. I've done so much wrong.

Even as a Christian everything I try to do that's right I do wrong. I hate myself. Dr. Peale I thought of getting rid of myself but I know that is not right. I sure could use some of your positive thinking right now. I always read how you give someone a card with a Scripture verse on it and it helps them. Do you have anything for me? I have read a lot of your books, but I can't seem to apply things to me. I am a negative thinker. I've been this way for quite some time. I would appreciate your help.

Thank you very much.

As requested, I did write a card for her. I suggested she carry it with her at all times and read it aloud frequently, especially just before going to sleep at night. I wanted to get belief thoughts working powerfully in her mind. Even if her disbelief in herself was deep-seated, I have found that such af-
tions, as the ones the following card contains,

often have a powerful effect. Here is the card I gave
her.

> I like me. I believe in me.
> I was created by God who never made
>   anything badly.
> His creation is wonderful
>   so I am wonderful.
> Divine perfection is within me.
>   I love life. I love people.
> I have ability. I can do things well.
>   I am happy. I am grateful.
> I treat myself with respect.
>   As a child of God, I believe in me.

The woman used this affirmation as directed and is
definitely emerging from her appalling self-depreciation.

When such personal disbelief exists, when there
is a lack of personality control, or when failure is
persistent, then the need for basic self-change is
indicated. It is utterly foolish to continue in such a
sorry state because it is a fact that self-change is
taking place in people every passing day. Such a
change of attitudes and conditions can occur in anyone. We can all change. I can change, and you too
can change.

My cousin, Lew Delaney, was a successful salesman who became the national sales manager for a
large company. Once we were talking about the
remarkable change that can take place in a person
and Lew said, "When a person is forthright about
himself or herself, honestly admits the need for

change, and then firmly sets about changing and has belief, that change will come. If he or she takes God into the process, that person can for sure change, and I mean change. Let me tell you about one of our salesmen named Tim. Did he change? Why, you wouldn't know him for the same man."

As Lew told me about him, I got the impression that Tim was a genial, likable man but lacking in force. He was, as Lew put it, the "lowest man on the totem pole," bottom salesman in production. As much as management hated to do it, Tim was about to be let go. Then to the surprise of everyone, Tim suddenly began to deliver. His sales mounted, and in one year's time he went from the bottom to the top one-third of the company's salesmen in productivity. At the end of the second year he was top man in sales nationally in the company. It seemed a miracle.

At the annual sales meeting when salesmen came together from all over the country, the president called Tim to the stage to receive the award for best salesman of the year. He ambled up, sort of embarrassed, and the president said, "I don't know when it has given me so much pleasure to make this award. Tim, you have become a truly great salesman, but even more you have become a truly great man. Actually you've got us all mystified. What a change in your record and in you! You just aren't the same Tim. Do you mind telling all the boys here how you did it?"

Lew said Tim was no public speaker, and he shifted from one foot to the other, became red in the face, and stammered in getting started. "Well," he said, "boss and fellows, I like you all and I think you'll understand. I was a failure, a flop, and I knew it. Nobody had to tell me. One night I said to myself, 'I don't want to be this way anymore,' and I got to thinking. I was sitting in our living room, and on the lower shelf in a bookcase I saw a Bible. I've got to admit I hadn't cracked it in years. Well, I got it out and at the front inside was written, 'To Tim. With love, Mama.' I just sat there leafing through it, and then a statement sort of leaped out at me that said I could change, that I could become a different man. And suddenly I just believed that.

"Well," continued Tim, "next morning I went downtown and bought myself a completely new outfit—a new suit, underwear, socks, shirt, shoes, tie—the works. Now I know the old saying that clothes don't make the man. But anyway I went back home and took a bath. I scrubbed my skin until it was red like a newborn baby's. I shampooed my head to get all those old negative thoughts out of my thick skull. Then I got dressed, and a new Tim went out selling. With God's help I started making sales, and I just kept on selling. Boss, I guess that's all there is to it."

Lew said, "It was unforgettable, fabulous! Those seven hundred men sat still a minute; then as one man they leaped to their feet, shouting and clapping and pounding each other on the back. It was pandemonium and," added Lew, "I've got to admit I was choked up and had tears in my eyes and so did just about everyone else."

And why not? A man had changed, become a new

man. So much so that you wouldn't have known him for the same person.

"Everyone wanted to know what the statement was that leaped out of the Bible to effect such a complete change in Tim," Lew said, "but nobody felt like asking since it was pretty private to Tim. But one day later when we were together, I asked him. He took his card and wrote 2 Corinthians 5:17 on the back. 'Look it up' was all he said. I was curious and did look it up. 'If anyone is in Christ, he is a new creation; old things have passed away; behold, all things have become new.'

"You know, Norman," said Lew, "you and I first heard that in Sunday school as kids back in Lynchburg [Ohio] and I never thought much about it. But do you know something? It really works. Tim's experience proves it."

How right he was—belief power gets powerful results.

In Chapter 3 we will discuss how to succeed in dealing with problems, and I hope this will be of real help to you.

3.

Success in Dealing with Problems

THE POSITIVE thinker is an achiever who gets powerful results for several reasons. He is not afraid of nor abashed by that phenomenon known as a problem. As a practical, positive-thinking philosopher, he knows that every problem contains the seeds of its own solution. If there are no problems, there will be no solutions and progress will stop. The positive thinker knows that good outcomes are rooted in the fertile soil of tough problems.

When the good Lord wants to give you some great value, how does He go about doing it? Does He wrap it up in an exotic package and hand it to you on a silver platter? Hardly. He is too subtle, too sophisticated for that. His method is much more adroit. He often buries that great value at the heart of a big, difficult problem. And how He must watch with delight to see if you have what it takes to break that problem apart and find at its heart, if you please, that pearl of great price.

41

But even so, wherever I go, either by direct statement or by implication, people seem to say, "Wouldn't life be simply wonderful if we had fewer problems, easier problems or, better still, no problems at all?" Would it?

I would like to answer this question by telling of an incident. Walking on Fifth Avenue in New York City, I saw a friend named George approaching. Judging from George's disconsolate and melancholy demeanor, I could see that he was not filled to overflowing with the ecstasy and exuberance of human existence. To put it more simply, George's spirit was dragging bottom.

This excited my sympathy so I asked him, "How are you, George?" For some minutes he meticulously enlightened me on how bad he felt. The more George talked, the worse I felt. "What has you so upset and discouraged?" I asked. This question really set him off.

"Oh, it's these problems," he fumed. "Problems and more problems, nothing but problems. I am fed up with problems." He became so exercised about the matter that he quite forgot to whom he was talking and lambasted these problems virulently, using in the process, I am sorry to report, a great many theological terms. But he certainly did not put them together in a theological manner. However, I understood what he meant all right, because he had "the ability to communicate."

"George," I said, breaking into his diatribe about his problems, "I would like to help you if possible. Tell me what I can do for you."

"Do for me?" he shouted. "Rid me of these problems. If you can do that, you will be my friend for life."

Since I always welcome an opportunity to become anyone's friend for life, I meditated upon George's situation until I finally came up with a solution. Although it may not have been the most pleasant suggestion, at least it was realistic. "George," I said, "let me get this straight. You want to be rid of your most difficult problems or perhaps most of your problems. But you are certainly not going to stand here on the street today and seriously tell me that you want to be rid of all your problems."

"The latter is what I want. I have had it," he insisted glumly.

"Okay. That being the case, I believe I can assist you. The other day, George, I was in a certain place on professional business, if I may thus characterize it. An official told me that approximately one hundred thousand people were there and not one of them had a problem."

The first glint of enthusiasm flashed in George's eyes and suffused his countenance as he eagerly exclaimed, "Boy, that's for me! Lead me to that place."

"You asked for it," I replied. "It's Woodlawn Cemetery."

That is a fact. No one in that or any cemetery has a problem. They couldn't care less what is reported in the newspapers, on television, or over the radio. They have no problems at all. But they are dead. Therefore, it is logical to assume that problems constitute a sign of life. I would go so far as to say that the more problems you have, the more alive you are. But if you have no problems at all, you are in great jeopardy. You are on the way out. I recommend that you pray to the Lord, saying, "Lord, what is the matter? Don't You trust me anymore? Give me some problems!"

The positive thinker is alive, alive mentally and spiritually, and knows that with the good Lord's help, he has what it takes to handle any problem that may arise in his lifetime. Good results are not obstructed by the fear that he is not capable of problem management. He attacks problems by intelligent thinking and, accordingly, gets positive results.

The concept of problems as suggested here would seem to indicate a mentally healthy attitude. Indeed one way of determining your state of mental health is to examine your reaction when a tough problem suddenly appears. Do you whine and complain that you are being unfairly put upon, petulantly asking, "Why me?" If that is the case, you might very well seek counseling in the hope of developing a more logical, philosophical understanding of difficulty. On the contrary, if you have a sturdy, clear-eyed mental attitude when a problem suddenly comes at you, then you will stand up to it fearlessly and confidently knowing that you have the capacity to handle it successfully. This attitude would seem to indicate the possession of good mental health. By this test the positive thinker has the quality of healthy-mindedness that enables him or her to bring positive results out of even the most difficult problems.

Some years ago the eminent psychiatrist, Dr. Smiley Blanton, and I founded the American Foundation of Religion and Psychiatry, the name of which was later changed to the Institutes of Religion and Health. As a result, I have been closely associated with psychiatrists and psychologists for many years. I respect them highly from a professional standpoint and hold them in affectionate regard as colleagues. We have had fun together as well as cooperated in exciting ventures.

A national convention of psychiatrists was held in a New York City hotel, and the lobby was constantly crowded with these doctors. Around the corner from the hotel is a big railroad station around which there are always huge flocks of pigeons. As far as anyone can determine, these are well-oriented, normal pigeons going about the daily functions of pigeons. But apparently the mental disorganization of the multitudes thronging in and out of the station finally transmitted itself to one of these pigeons. By a process that has never been accounted for, this pigeon presently found itself in the lobby of the nearby hotel, flying around among the psychiatrists. In fact, it is reliably reported that this pigeon flew around for two whole days before any psychiatrist would admit to another that he saw a pigeon!

But, however that may be, our clinic has had considerable success in giving many people the great blessing of a healthy-minded attitude toward problems and the constructive know-how to handle them successfully. In this clinic we have dealt with just about every known human problem. You name it, we have seen it.

One problem is worry that besets multitudes of persons. Worry is not to be minimized as a personality problem. The English word *worry,* I am told, is derived from an Anglo-Saxon word, *wyrgan,* which literally meant "to choke or strangle." If someone seized you about the throat, pressing with maximum strength, he would be dramatically doing to you what you do to yourself if you are a victim of worry for a long period. You are, in effect, literally strangling or choking your own creative powers.

Among the hieroglyphics revealed during excavations on a cliff in Britain was a rough drawing chiseled out of the rock depicting a huge wolf sinking its teeth into the throat of a man. This drawing was deciphered as the ancients' effort to illustrate worry. It seems that way back in the misty past people were plagued by that devastating, self-destroying emotional problem we call worry.

Another personal problem we often see is that of fear. It may be described as worry in-depth. In addition, there is that of anxiety. What is anxiety? A dark, irrational, conflicting, and terrifying feeling that something awful may happen. The late Dr. Smiley Blanton used to say that "anxiety is America's greatest plague."

The Institutes of Religion and Health also deal with marital, alcohol, drug, and youth problems and many other situations that frustrate the free, creative flow of human potential. But perhaps the most common difficulty besetting modern, educated, and highly organized persons generally is the inability to cope with the ordinary problems of human existence.

A most viable procedure for developing a person well able to cope is turning him into a person of faith. Faith is the greatest of all therapies, barring none. Faith in what? In God, in people, in your job, and in yourself. When an individual develops strong faith and when doubt and attitudes of inadequacy are minimized or even eliminated, that person no longer has any serious problem with coping. That person becomes thoroughly changed in his mental and spiritual nature. A former weakness becomes a strength. The result is that a previously inadequate person can now undertake and handle problems with verve and power. Problems that formerly overwhelmed, frustrated, and defeated him no longer do so. Now he surmounts them. He solves them or becomes philosophically able to live with them. And he does so with the positive attitude that instead of being obstacles, problems are actually career builders, super know-how producers.

I had to go through this change in mental attitude myself. As a young man I was anything but a positive thinker. In fact, I had a dominating inferiority complex. Learning how to shake it off and live normally was one of the greatest problems I ever had to face in life. I had some ambitious dreams and set big goals. I had boundless enthusiasm and energy. But I was plagued by self-doubt and feelings of inadequacy. I endured the sneering message from my subconscious: "You can't do it, you haven't got what it takes."

For example, one of my goals, my chief goal really, was to be a public speaker. But the mere thought of appearing before an audience frightened me. When I did attempt it, my knees shook, my mouth was dry, and I hesitated ineffectively. Still I wanted to speak in public; I miserably desired to do so. I felt strongly motivated to do things, to accomplish objectives, and to realize ambitions. If you ever wanted to do something and believed that you could not, longed to be somebody and yet had a self-doubting attitude, then you had a problem. And that problem, of course, hatched a lot of other problems. How could you possibly handle situations in your life and make good decisions if you were a defeated disbeliever in yourself?

I was fortunate in encountering four men in my youth who helped me with myself. The first was Ben Arneson, a professor at Ohio Wesleyan University. He saw and understood my pathetic dilemma. One day he said, "Peale, please remain after class." He sat studying me. "What's the matter with you, Norman? I know you work hard and have mastered the material in this course, but you never speak up unless I call upon you. And then your face gets red, you flounder and stammer. You are embarrassed and self-conscious. Why? Tell me why?"

He did not give me time to try to come up with an excuse. "I know why. You have an inferiority complex that you've been nursing until it dominates you. Actually you are egotistical in thinking that everyone is watching you, that you are the center of attention." He sat bouncing an eraser up and down on his desk. Suddenly he said, "See that eraser? A wonderful thing, an eraser. It can rub out mistakes, make the paper clean." And hurling it against the desk, "Look at the bounce it's got built into it.

"Same thing with you, son. Wipe out that inferiority attitude, get the bounce going that almighty God built into you." He continued along this line, "You've been reared in a godly home to have faith, and faith can always cancel out fear. And you've got fear—the fear to live, to be your own good self. Take it up with the Lord, Norman. Let the good Lord remake you. He will if you ask Him."

I stumbled down the hall with a mixture of feelings. Anger was one. Frustration was another, but a strange emerging hope was there also. Walking down the long flight of stairs, I stopped on the fourth step from the bottom. I remember it precisely because on that step one of the major events of my life occurred. I knew the professor was right about what I was and what I could be, if——! Fortunately I knew what to do. I prayed, "Dear Lord, I have seen You change bad people into good people. I have seen You change drunks into sober men and women, and thieves into honest persons. Can't You also change a poor defeated boy like me into a normal person? Please do, dear Lord." I really meant those words I prayed.

James Russell Lowell in his poem "The Cathedral" wrote:

I, that still pray at morning and at eve . . .
Thrice in my life perhaps have truly prayed,
Thrice, stirred below my conscious self, have
felt
That perfect disenthralment which is God.

Those lines perfectly describe what happened to me in that unforgettable moment. But there was no apparent miracle except that I felt strangely peaceful and happy.

One day another professor named William E. Smyser kept me after class. "Norman," he said, "here are two books I want you to read." One was the *Meditations of Marcus Aurelius,* the other *The Sayings of Ralph Waldo Emerson* edited by Bruce Perry. "They will help you to understand the greatness inherent in the human mind when faith is dominantly present in the thoughts." Many times since then I have stood by that magnificent statue of Marcus Aurelius on the Capitoline Hill in Rome and tried to thank him for all he did for me in helping me develop that normal self-confidence I call positive thinking.

The struggle to solve my personal problem of inferiority was certainly not an easy or a short one. A deep-seated problem may require lots of time and patience and stick-to-it-iveness to get positive results. The perseverance to hang in there in the tussle with a tough problem is of the utmost importance. The tendency to accept defeat will strongly resist this ousting process, but the problem must be attacked repeatedly with positive thoughts and faith until it gives way, as it assuredly will, if one has the will and fortitude never to give up.

Perhaps six years after that experience on the college steps, I was the young pastor of a church in the Blackstone Valley of Rhode Island. The going was tough because of a long strike at the New England textile mills and a divided congregation. All this I was trying to heal and deal with. My old self-doubt began once again to emerge, but I had the rare good fortune to have a wise and discerning friend, a man of strong and rugged faith, a real positive thinker. His name was Rob Rowbottom. Listening to my negative remarks, he came up with a statement that has lived powerfully in my mind ever since. It was one of the wisest utterances I have ever heard in my lifetime. Rob simply said, "Never build a case against yourself."

Write those six words on a card, and carry it with you every day. Better still, write those words indelibly upon your mind. With that positive thought going for you, no problem you will ever face can be too much for you.

Still I struggled with the problem of myself. It is a fact that of all the problems we ever have to deal with, the problem of the self is often the most complex, difficult, and tenacious. But if we solve that one, all other problems become immeasurably less difficult.

Approximately ten years after the experience on the college steps, I was the young, inexperienced pastor of an outstanding church near a university campus, the University Methodist Church of Syracuse, New York. It had a beautiful edifice, but the congregation had declined and the financial debt had increased. I might add that it seems I have always been favored with difficult jobs. I say favored because the bottom is a most advantageous place. The only direction one can go from the bottom is up. And at the beginning of my incumbency this church was at the bottom. Once again that old die-hard feeling of inadequacy began to reemerge. The whole enterprise became, in my thinking, a horrendous problem. My entire view was dominated by what I viewed as a mountainous difficulty.

Again fortune favored me. In my congregation was one of the greatest businessmen Syracuse ever had. His name was Harlow B. Andrews. He was said to have been one of the early inventors of the dishwasher. He operated one of the first supermarkets in the United States, bringing in fresh fruit and vegetables from Florida and California by express train and selling them off season in prime condition four days later on Salina Street. He was a very religious man, head of the Syracuse Rescue Mission, but he had the fastest team of trotting horses in Syracuse and would race them down James Street in summer and on frozen Onondaga Lake in winter. A local banker once commented that Andrews had the most acute financial sense of anyone in town, that all he had to do was extend his fingers and money sprang to them. I was so fascinated that I cultivated his company assiduously in the hope of acquiring his gift but, alas, I had no success.

So I took my problem or problems to this pious,

wise, and astute man. He listened as I outlined all
the difficulties in the situation. Finally when I had
run down a bit, he asked, "Is that all of your problem?" I nodded, whereupon he waved his hands in a
sweeping motion as though he were piling up a lot
of stuff. "Quite a pile," he grinned. "Sure is a big
problem, isn't it?" Then he said, "Come here, son,
let's walk around this problem," and he made as
though to poke at the pile. Fascinated, I noticed his
rough big forefinger. He had arthritis in that finger, causing it to be crooked, but he could point
mighty straight with that crooked finger.

"Every problem," he said, "has a soft spot. I've
learned that fact over the years and don't you give
me an argument about it. Every problem has a soft
spot. When you find it, the problem can be broken
apart, and you can put a right solution together."
So he proceeded to walk around the problem, muttering to himself. Then, "Ah, we've got it. Here is
that soft spot," meanwhile wiggling that forefinger
into it. "Let's handle it at this point. This is the
essence of your difficulties. Let's take it from here
and go forward." Then he added, "Apply some positive faith. Believe, believe, believe. Pray big prayers,
have a big faith, get some big ideas. See yourself
getting big results. Go to it, son, with God's help.
You've got what it takes." As I started to leave, he
pointed that big old finger at me. "And in the name
of God, believe in yourself." What this unforgettable character was whimsically saying is that positive thinkers get powerful results.

Some years ago the head of one of the largest

industrial corporations in this country made an appointment to see me. I had often heard of this man and read of his activities, but I had never met him. When he came into my office, I at once sensed the force of his personality. I realized that no one could have attained his eminence in the business world without great mental capacity and lots of talent.

But Mr. X, as I shall call him, was very shaken and showed symptoms of a nervous breakdown. He explained that his doctor ascribed his deteriorating emotional and physical condition to pressure and overstress. He told me that he had read one of my books and lately had been attending Sunday services at the church. Both the book and the talks had been helpful to him, he indicated. Then he came up with a unique suggestion. "When I do not feel up to par physically, I consult my doctor, and he gives me a prescription. So now that I am in a bad way emotionally and maybe also spiritually, why can't I come to you as a mental and spiritual doctor? Please study my case and write me a prescription. I have faith in you, and I promise I will follow it."

In our conversation I learned that he had become terrified of making decisions concerning the important problems facing him almost daily as president and chief executive officer of his corporation. This reaction astonished him by its unaccountability. Previously he had been keen-minded and quick and accurately decisive. In some way the pressure under which he had broken had resulted in a mind-

gripping fear that he would decide problems erro-
neously. As a result, he had become timorous and
indecisive. Aides, forced to cover for him, had pro-
tected his position thus far, but sadly he said, "I
know I can't get away much longer with my inability to deal with problems."

One must handle people with sensitivity and with
whatever know-how one may have picked up by
study and experience. I had several meetings with
this man and became convinced that by restoring
his once-positive thought processes, he could be
healed. Since the reason he came to me, a minister,
was due to his religious inclinations, I would treat
him on that basis.

"Well, Mr. X," I said, "I believe that if you add
deep mental peace to your mind, your drive will be
enhanced and confidence in your judgments will be
restored." I quoted those great lines from the poet
Edwin Markham: "At the heart of the cyclone tear-
ing the sky is a place of central calm." That is to
say, the cyclone or elemental power draws its force
from a calm center. A human being, in the mind,
derives power from central calmness. "Now I prescribe for you the following daily affirmations":

1. The peace of God that passes all understanding is in my mind and my body now.
2. I am not alone. The Lord is by my side and
   all day long He will be near me.
3. God will help me with every decision; and
   since there is no error in the Lord, wrong
   things will be removed from my mind.

4. I believe that God is guiding me. I receive that guidance. I will act upon it without hesitation.

"When you retire at night, thank the Lord for being with you. Know that you have decided rightly. Then go to sleep in peace."

"That makes sense," he said thoughtfully. He folded the paper on which I had written this prescription under an Rx to make it more authoritative. "I'll follow it." And he did regularly and completely. It was not too long before he was his old competent self again.

A long time later the head of a big soft drink company said, "Thanks for pulling me out of a mental funk." When I expressed surprise, he pulled a paper from his wallet. I was astonished to see the prescription I'd given Mr. X. "He passed copies of that around among his friends," he explained. "You see, he is a real positive thinker. And he says to be a positive thinker, you've got to have the peace of God in your mind because then you are afraid of nothing. Isn't that something?" He added, "But it does work, it really does."

As I said early in this chapter, a positive thinker is never afraid of nor abashed by a problem. He knows that problems contain solutions, and the tougher the problem, the tougher he must be. Better results will be attained by tackling the problem resolutely and intelligently.

My longtime friend, George Cullum, Sr., whose firm laid much of the underground piping at the

Dallas-Fort Worth Airport, said, "When we strike tough hard rock, we simply get tougher and harder than the rock." Naturally George was always a thoroughgoing positive thinker. It has often been demonstrated that a tough problem, when met head-on with courage and with positive anticipation of success, will yield greater results than a soft or easy problem.

Branch Rickey, one-time head successively of the Saint Louis Cardinals, the old Brooklyn Dodgers, and the Pittsburgh Pirates baseball clubs, told me admiringly about the famous player Stan Musial. Branch said that he asked the outstanding hitter how he had attained his high batting average. Musial replied, "I always wait for the tough pitch. I like the tough pitch best because when you connect with it squarely, it goes, really goes."* So too when you and I are not afraid of a tough one but stand up to it and resolutely swing at it, we are very likely to connect with it squarely. Then we go, really go.

I often think of my old friend R. P. Ettinger. He was my publisher until his death. Some rated him as one of the most capable businessmen in New York. He lost his voice due to cancer and could no longer speak. One day his wife called me. "Dick wants you to talk to him. Remember he published your book, *The Power of Positive Thinking*. Just say something to encourage him."

"Hello, R. P.," I said, "do you know something? I think you're just about positive thinker number

* From *The American Diamond.* Copyright © 1965 by Branch Rickey and Roger Riger. Reprinted by permission of Simon & Schuster.

one. And even more important, God loves you. He knows you can handle a problem, for you have a tough, strong faith. You've always gotten big results out of big problems, and you will do the same out of this one."

He told me years later that those words from a friend who loved him and believed in him "brought him out of it." And when one day I heard him make a thrilling talk to a large group in a rather husky but clear voice, it was another powerful demonstration of the fact that some positive thinkers get powerful results.

As head of the Chicago Bears, George Halas won more football games in his career than the legendary Alonzo Stagg. He was the only man the famous Vince Lombardi would embrace, the only one he would call Coach. George Halas had a large framed sign in his office and a similar one in his bedroom— "Never go to bed a loser." That's great. And here is one that is perhaps just as good—"Always get up a winner." As we follow these two mottoes, we too may be positive thinkers who get powerful results. We will turn problems into good outcomes.

The negative thinker does a very dangerous thing. Constantly, this person pumps out negative thoughts about everything. Accordingly, the world around him is activated negatively. There is a law, the law of attraction, that like attracts like. The old saying, "Birds of a feather flock together," sums this up. Thoughts of a kind have a mutual affinity. Send out negative thoughts, and negative results will return. It is an immutable law of mind, of cause and effect.

The positive thinker, on the other hand, sets very different forces in motion. He sends out robust thoughts of faith, hope, and optimism. Positive thoughts flow vigorously from his mind, and the world around him is activated positively. On the basis of the same law of attraction, positive results come surging back to the positive thinker. This process also is a law of mind. It is the way life works.

How fortunate one is to learn and use this creative process of positive thinking early in life! But it can be learned and applied to good effect at any age. I received a letter from a ninety-three-year-old man, a lifelong attorney-at-law. He said:

> I have had an inferiority complex all my life for 93 years. [It's the longest one I ever heard of.] But I read your book and I believed it. I put it into practice and want to report that I have finally made an end to my inferiority complex. Thank you very much.

But the P.S. was the payoff. "P.S. The future looks great."

Turn now to the next chapter. We are going to talk about the positive thinker as an achiever.

4.

The Positive Thinker as an Achiever

"I'M JUST a country boy working at positive thinking," he said with a shy smile. "Mind if I walk along with you a ways?" He explained that he had been reading motivational books for several years and seemed proud of his collection. "The first one I read was your *Power of Positive Thinking*. Mom gave it to me for Christmas when I was a kid, and I was sort of brought up on it. I'm trying to believe that I can reach my ambition."

"And what may that be?" I asked.

"I want to be a lawyer and maybe get into politics, but that all seems like a dream that can't ever come true."

"Why can't it come true?"

"Because we're poor. And you have to go to college and law school to be a lawyer. Nobody in my family ever went to college. We're just farm folks up country."

This conversation took place as I was walking

back to my hotel. I had just given a speech at a motivational rally which was packed mostly by ambitious young men and women working in sales.

My companion said, "I'm nineteen years old, and when I saw in the paper about this meeting, I came down by bus. Cost nearly my last buck. I watched you leave the hall after your talk and followed you. Tell me that you think I can make it. Just tell me that and give me some pointers on how I can reach my goal."

It was all rather pathetic, yet inspiring too. He really touched me. He was so traditionally American. A poor boy wanting to be a lawyer and to get involved in his country's life.

"You have all the makings," I said. "You have intensity of desire, a definite goal, a worthy purpose. You have shown perseverance by coming to this meeting by bus, using up your few dollars. You have a good mind, for there is intelligence shining out of your eyes. You say you are working at faith. So believe you can. With God's help, there is no doubt that you can be what you want to be."

I took a pad from my pocket and wrote these words: "I can do all things through Christ who strengthens me. Philippians 4:13." Then I asked, "Are you a believer in God?"

"Oh, yes, I believe."

"Well, belief and a positive thought pattern are the secrets along with hard work, determination, and imaging your goal." I pointed to the words I'd written. "Saturate your mind with those words. That will help a lot."

He went off with a swinging gait. I watched until he rounded the corner on his way to the bus station for the long trip up country. He waved to me. It may reveal sentiment on my part when I confess that I had a catch in my throat. Our country is still the same wonderful America where youths can follow their dreams. That my young friend will make it I haven't the slightest doubt.

It seems that everywhere I go I encounter men and women, young and old, who are working on goals and on self-improvement. And I must admit that they help build up my own motivation.

In the Atlanta airport I ran into an old friend, a business executive, and we had a stimulating conversation about positive thinking and how it changes people into goal achievers. On the back of his business card, he had written that the *positive principle* is the mental and spiritual process by which a person moves from self-limitation, deterioration, and failure to self-improvement, growth, and accomplishment.

When a person is not succeeding as well as desired, it only makes sense that some change is indicated. And often, perhaps usually, such a failing person assumes that the solution to the problem is to change jobs. But actually the better way may be not to change the job but to change the person. A changed individual may make the job altogether different. The job may become a remarkable opportunity instead of continuing to be the dead end it seems. A changed person often results in a changed everything. Mental and spiritual alteration may be just the process that will carry a changed person to a success he wouldn't have dreamed possible before the personal change took place.

At a sales motivational meeting, a young man said, "I go for this positive-thinking stuff, but I have a stupid, lousy job. What do I do about that?"

"You know something," I said, "you might have the opportunity of a lifetime in that job you put down. You might be able to become one of the top executives of your organization if instead of depreciating what you are doing and instead of wanting to change jobs, you really changed yourself. Do that and maybe you will change what you call a 'stupid, lousy job' into an exciting one. Why not visualize yourself as exactly the kind of man your employer thinks you are? He wouldn't have you in that job unless he thought you could handle it. He is pretty smart in his insights into personality qualities. Maybe he actually knows you better than you know yourself. Practice liking everyone, and deliberately start liking your job. I'm guessing you will soon have a better time at work. Do this, and you will start moving up."

Basically he was a disbeliever in himself. That seemed obvious. But I sold him on what he really was underneath and on what he could do. Fortunately he was goal oriented, but he seemed mentally disorganized and pretty negative. "I'm not really a positive person," he explained. "How the boss ever got the impression that I am mystifies me."

"He probably sizes you up as a potentially outgoing and motivated individual," I suggested. "Anyway, did you ever hear of the 'as if' principle? I explain it to everyone."

He shook his head, "No, that's a new one on me."

"Well, it's a sound psychological principle, one that can really change people, provided they want change to take place. It was, I believe, first stated by William James, who is often labeled the father of American psychology. It means that if a person is dissatisfied with himself as he is or with his job, he may image himself as he wishes to be and the job as a terrific opportunity. Then he acts as if he and the job were that. If he persists in this alteration effort, the strong psychological and spiritual forces inherent in his personality structure or in his nature will conspire to make him and his job just that."

I explained that I had seen the "as if" principle put into effective action so often by people who want to change that I had strong faith in its efficacy. He listened with growing interest as I told him of dull, unenthusiastic men and women whom I had persuaded to act as if they were enthusiastic. In due course, they actually took on enthusiastic attributes. And I told him of others who were shy and introverted, who deliberately acted as if they were extraverted and outgoing, and who ultimately became genuinely that kind of individual.

Well, he seemed to get the message, and fortunately he didn't overdo it. Next morning he did not go bounding into the office breathing out joy and enthusiasm. He continued to be low-key, but he began to take a real interest in his assignment and in his associates, especially in the shy ones who are in every group. He went out of his way to talk with them. He encouraged those who seemed to be feeling down and depressed. But the main thing is that he gradually got beyond his old gripy self, and in acting as if he were a positive, caring, and outgoing person, he gradually became one in fact. I saw him only once after that when I spoke at a national convention of his industry. He introduced himself and told me of the minor executive position he was then holding. Here was a man who had experienced alteration and, as a result, was now gaining on goals that formerly had seemed far beyond him.

It is pathetic that so many people who could do a terrific job in life just don't do it. Instead they settle apathetically for something less. The famous writer James M. Barrie stated the matter very well: "The most gladsome thing in the world is that few of us fall very low; the saddest that, with such capabilities, we seldom rise high." Perhaps another way of saying it is that we are self-made victims of mediocrity. We make ourselves content to be what amounts to mediocre when the actual fact is that we do not need to be that at all.

Why does a person fail to become what he or she could be? There are probably many answers to that question, but a simple one is that the person doesn't give the job or the effort the whole mind and doesn't let the entire self become involved. It has always been true that the world gives itself to the all-outs and denies itself to the half-outs.

When I think of the goal achievers I have known,

they all had certain characteristics in common. Always, without exception, they had a goal, not an indefinite, indistinct, fuzzy objective, but a sharp, clearly defined goal. They knew precisely what they wanted, and they went for that goal with focused determination and unremitting effort. They all had enthusiasm, a burning, glowing enthusiasm, and it was sustained through all manner of difficulty. These high achievers never gave up, no matter how tough the going. Add up all the positive qualities, and these achievers had them all. Then the big plus was that they were all believers. Every day all the way they never doubted; they were never negative thinkers. All the goal achievers I have ever known have been positive thinkers who got powerful results.

In Chicago you will see the name Rubloff on building after building all over town. Arthur Rubloff is one of the greatest real estate men in this or any country. He made North Michigan Avenue one of the notable thoroughfares of the world, known everywhere as "The Magnificent Mile." He was the innovator of the shopping center—his Evergreen Plaza is a spectacular example of a free enterprise restoration of the inner city.

Arthur is an art collector, a philanthropist sharing his wealth for the benefit of all people. He had no rich father and no help along the road to the top. He got there on his own; he sold newspapers, shined shoes, and worked as a galley boy on a Great Lakes freighter. He was a poor boy with a dream and a goal plus the willingness to work. Add to that formula the will never to give up, enthusiasm for life, intelligence, positive thinking, always positive thinking, and he had the makings of successful achievement.

Also from Chicago is another famous goal achiever, W. Clement Stone, who began in the classic Horatio Alger pattern as a poverty-stricken kid selling newspapers on the South Side. He is now worth, so they say, a third of a billion dollars. Also a generous philanthropist, Stone has given his life to motivating others to become what they have within themselves to be.

In an article in his magazine *Success,* Clem Stone says to ignore those who dolefully say you can't. He offers some wise advice on how to give the lie to the "it can't be done" excuse. Here is what he says:

> Millions of people in every walk of life have never tried to achieve high goals that were achievable or solve problems that were solvable. Why? They were told or believed "It can't be done." And they never learned or applied that essence of the art of motivation with a positive mental attitude (PMA) that could have helped them achieve any goal that didn't violate universal laws, the laws of God, and the rights of their fellowmen.
>
> They could have achieved the highest goals and solved the most difficult problems:
>
> ... If they had motivated themselves to Recognize, Relate, Assimilate, and Apply from what they read, heard, saw, thought and experienced. . . .
>
> ... If they had set high desirable goals,

written them down, engaged in concentrated study, thinking, and planning time for a half hour or more daily on their goals. The subconscious will come up with the answers through repetition, repetition, repetition.*

I frequently stay overnight with my longtime friend John W. Galbreath at his 4,400-acre farm, Darby Dan, near Columbus, Ohio. John has led in the remaking of the downtown and river front areas of the city and has built huge installations in all parts of the world, notably the great Mei Foo section of Hong Kong. He was the owner of the Pittsburgh Pirates baseball club.

Galbreath was born on a poor twenty-acre farm on the outskirts of Mount Sterling, Ohio, and as did all American kids prior to the school-bus era, he trudged to school on foot. A lovable, outgoing person, he preserves, in older years after achieving great success, the same down-to-earth humility that has always characterized him. But along with this self-effacement is a sharp, keen mind that led him from poverty to a high-level position in the world. The country boy who came out of poverty is now the friend of presidents and Queen Elizabeth II.

When he takes off from his private airport on Darby Dan Farm, the flight path often takes him over the stony twenty acres where he grew up as a boy and where his father struggled to wrest a few dollars from the soil to support his family. How was

*Reprinted with permission. © 1983 Success Unlimited.

this miracle of achievement attained? John Galbreath will tell you that it was done first by desire, intense desire. That is his basic formula for goal achieving—intensity of desire. To that he has added a humble faith in God, an upright character, and an outgong interest in people who today strive to do him honor, not because of his riches, but because of what he is—an honorable, lovable, humble, and very able human being. His story, like the others I've mentioned and scores of others I would like to mention, is that of a positive thinker—a positive thinker who set goals and reached them. I'm sure he would unhesitatingly tell you that you can be a goal achiever too if you follow the basic principles laid out in this book.

To reach a goal an individual has to have a strong motivating force as well as an intense desire and the belief that it can be done. While I was writing this chapter, Abraham Spector, a longtime friend and associate, came into my office. He is an outstanding CPA, a leader in his profession. I have worked with Abe as a personal adviser for a good many years. He is a real achiever. So I put the question to him, "Abe, what made you a successful man? Did you have a goal?"

He replied, "I was born in the Bronx and grew up there in a poor family. I don't use the word *poverty*. That's a later term. But back then we were poor people, a poor Jewish family. And," Abe hesitated, then continued, "I just didn't want to be poor anymore."

How many Americans have been motivated by

being poor as Abe Spector was? Legions of them. Another Abe, Abe Lincoln was poor, very poor. Americans hate poverty. Lincoln's mother said to her son, "Abe, be somebody." I was of a poor family myself. Being poor causes hardships, but it has been one of the great American motivators. It has stimulated many to rise higher, to become achievers in life. They didn't want to be poor anymore, so they developed goals and became positive thinkers. They worked and worked and thought and thought and believed and believed. They built their lives on the "of course you can" principle, and they attained their goals. They were activated by strong motivational force.

One of the greatest demonstrations of how a motivated positive thinker reaches goals is the story of the unforgettable Olympic champion Jesse Owens. I had the privilege of personally knowing this superb athlete, this great American. Some sports writers judged him to be one of the greatest athletes in the history of this country. Jesse Owens himself vigorously disclaimed such high evaluation, but there is no doubt about his athletic prowess or about his greatness as a sincere Christian and as a notable human being.

One evening during a dinner program of the Ohio Newspaper Publishers' Association in Columbus, Ohio, I sat by Jesse Owens at the head table. I got him to talk about his life and career, and he related the following story. He was born into a black family of extremely limited means. "We were poor materially but rich spiritually." He also said that as a young boy, he was slight of build, even skinny, with a below-average physique. But his believing, positive mother told him that he was destined to do great things in life, that he was going to be somebody. He didn't see how that was possible. His family was poor and had no influence. Everything seemed against him, but his mother kept reminding him of the Lord by saying, "You just be a believer and keep faithful. You will be led."

One day at a school assembly the speaker was Charlie Paddock, one of the most famous athletes of the time. On many a sports page he was hailed as "the fastest human being alive." I saw him run once in the Boston Arena, and he was like greased lightning. Having long since retired from his athletic career, Paddock gave his time to motivating kids everywhere, and he had a tremendous influence on youths.

Over a thousand kids packed the school auditorium that day to hear the renowned runner speak, and little Jesse Owens was on the front row. Owens said that Charlie Paddock walked to the front of the stage, put both hands in his hip pockets, let a deep silence fall, and in a full strong voice shot out the question, "Do you know who you are? You don't, eh? Well, I'm here to tell you. You are Americans, and you are the children of God. You can be somebody. You can be anything you want to be if you have a goal and will work and believe and have good moral character. You really can be what you want to be with the help of the good God."

Jesse Owens told me that in that moment, in a

flash, he knew just what he wanted to be; his goal was instantly formed. He wanted to be the next Charlie Paddock, the fastest human being alive. He could scarcely wait for the speech to end, and immediately he rushed up and clasped Paddock's hand. With a touch of awe in his voice, he told me, "When I grabbed Charlie's hand, an electric impulse passed up my arm and through my body."

Then he rushed to the coach, shouting, "Coach, I have a dream, I have a dream. I'm going to be the next Charlie Paddock. I'm going to be the fastest man on earth!" The coach was a wise man, a motivator and guide. He put his arm around the shoulders of the frail little boy. "That's right, Jesse. Have a dream, a big dream. You will never go any higher than you can dream. But you can go as high as you dream if you work at it, believe in it, and stick to it. To reach your dream, you must climb a ladder on which there are four rungs. Mark them well. They are (1) determination, (2) dedication, (3) discipline, and (4) attitude."

The coach went on to say that attitude is of primary importance, even more than the other three qualities taken together, because attitude deals with how a person thinks and believes. And before anyone can be determined, dedicated, and disciplined, he must make a mental and spiritual commitment to the goal. He must continue to think positively about it all the way to its attainment.

I was fascinated as Jesse Owens told me this story of his awakening to his possibilities, his goal, his dream and how it could come true. What fol-

THE POSITIVE THINKER AS AN ACHIEVER

lowed? He thrilled the world in the 1936 Olympic Games by winning four gold medals. He tied the record for the one-hundred-meter race and ran the two-hundred-meter race faster than it had ever been run before. His broad jump record set in the games lasted for twenty-two years, and his performance on the relay team was spectacular. And finally, when the American Hall of Athletic Fame was established, the name that led all the rest was that of the frail little boy from Cleveland who followed a dream, a goal to athletic immortality. Reflect on the story of Jesse Owens and know, really know in your heart, that you too as a positive thinker can reach your goal.

To help you do just that, here are ten "of course you can" principles. Engrave them on your mind. Believe they will work when used. By applying them, the positive thinker gets powerful results.

1. Stamp your goal indelibly on your mind.
2. Always image yourself as succeeding with God's help.
3. When a negative thought enters your mind, immediately cancel it out with a positive thought.
4. Mentally minimize difficulties; maximize your strengths.
5. Deny the power of difficulty over you. Affirm the power of faith to overcome.
6. Believe in yourself.
7. Always be genuinely friendly.
8. Keep on learning, growing, improving yourself.

9. Build a ladder to your dreams—
   Determination
   Dedication
   Discipline
   Attitude
10. Every day practice the greatest of all positive affirmations, "I can do all things through Christ who strengthens me."

But let's face it, the problems of life can gang up on us. Difficult situations develop out of various causes. A temporary letdown of positive attitudes could be one. So, in the next chapter we will explore an important issue—how to make things go better for you.

5.

You Can Make Things Go Better

"SHOOT FOR the moon. Even if you miss it, you'll land among the stars." So said Les Brown, a former member of a state legislature but now a popular youth motivational speaker.

"A big shot is a little shot who keeps on shooting," declared Stanley Kresge, a prominent Detroit philanthropist.

One man says aim high, the other keep it going. Both principles are basic in knowing how to make things go better for you.

When things are not going well for you, ask yourself whether you are thinking good things or bad. It is a well-established fact that there is a strong tendency for outward manifestations to match inner thought patterns. Thoughts are alive and produce vibratory influence. They have acute drawing power. It is summertime as I write this, and last evening a friend complained that he just cannot be out-of-doors on a summer evening because he "draws all the mosquitoes in the county." I do not claim that thinking draws mosquitoes (though it could just be), but it is a fact that nonpositive thinking draws nonpositive results which can cause more trouble than mosquitoes ever did.

I knew a man once who had attained some success, but a recession adversely affected the industry in which he was an employee. Many workers had to be laid off, and he was among them, temporarily he was told. Something happened to his spirit as the layoff continued and he was reduced to dire financial straits. Finally he had to take a low-status job, and he was lucky to get it. It was all he could find to bring in some money to care for his wife and children. His negative attitude deepened, triggered perhaps by the fact that his brother was a distinguished and successful, even famous, man. But he plugged away and did a good job.

I was in his city on a speaking engagement, and he found me in the coffee shop of the motel where I was staying. It seems that he had read one of my books and felt that perhaps I could help him. His immediate problem, he said, was that one of his children was ready for college and the others were just a few years behind. The question was, how was he ever going to be able to put them through college? After all he was the "no-account failure in his family" while his brother was "a big shot success."

"Just what does your brother's success have to do with this problem?" I asked "It's you and your children we are talking about."

"Oh, I'm a flop, always was. My brother has all the brains. He gets all the breaks in life."

"You need a larger income, don't you?" He nodded. I continued, "You have just stated several reasons why you do not gain the required increased resources. One is that you are not competing with yourself but with your brother. Another is self-depreciation, always putting yourself down. Don't you know that there is a tendency for all of us to be taken at our own self-appraisal? I suggest that you start holding yourself in higher respect and you might also start being proud of your brother. Generosity toward him will actually activate a flow of generosity and prosperity toward you."

Obviously this man possessed more ability than he realized, but he had been putting himself down for so long that he had come to believe he was second-rate. He was a confirmed self-depreciator. Daily he was violating one of the basic principles of success—never build a case against yourself. This man's self-image had been so constantly self-tarnished that he had mentally come to assume a picture of himself as a complete failure. This mass of negativism had been compounded by his resentment of his brother's success. Mentally he was in competition with his brother and had developed a built-in failure attitude that took refuge in a no-ability, no-account concept of himself. Yet there was enough lingering hope still flickering in his mind to bring him to consult someone who he thought might provide some help.

I suggested a plan for him, and he followed it. It

helped to get him started on the road to a successful life. The first step had to do with his attitudes toward his brother, himself, and his job. He was to stop being jealous of his brother and to quit competing with him in his mind. Instead he was to get into real competition with himself. He was to image himself as daily doing a better job. This meant challenging himself, believing in himself, and definitely visualizing successful achievement.

I encouraged him to list on paper all his assets of personality, intelligence, experience, and native ability, to compel him to recognize himself as a somebody instead of as a nobody, his current self-appraisal. Such self-image psychology, when developed, has the power to create a rational self-knowledge and lead to normal self-confidence. This man's basic quality was indicated by his ability to discard the crutch of self put-down and venture into a healthy-minded self-esteem. He learned to believe in himself in a normal manner.

Gradually he developed a good feeling about his brother. They grew closer together, and ultimately a mutually caring relationship resulted. As healthy-mindedness increased and with it self-esteem, people regarded him more highly, and the final outcome was a higher position. Naturally this sequence of self-improvement did not work out overnight. It seldom does that quickly. The emergence from sickly negativism and self-depreciation does not come speedily or easily. But once a person wants self-improvement, devises a plan, and follows it sincerely, the desired result will come. Things will go better because the person is becoming better.

Just one sequel to this fascinating story of a once-defeated man who must remain nameless because of my promise to him. It concerns his original problem about getting his children through college during the tough time of his personal reconstruction. I suggested the principle of imaging or visualization. He was to picture each child in turn entering college as a well-prepared student, to "see" each of them working to help pay the costs, and to hold the picture of each going forward in cap and gown on commencement day to receive her diploma.

"I don't know, indeed will never know, how we did it," he told me a long time later. "But all of us held the 'image,' and things just worked out. It was a miracle," he concluded wonderingly.

"You practiced scientific positive principles of thought and attitude," I said. "And because of your strong religious faith, you had the power of spirit going for you." This man and his entire family found the priceless secret of making things go better, much better.

When things are not going well for you and you are looking for ways to make them go better, here is another procedure I urge you to consider. Start and continue practicing the amazing law of supply. It will work miracles in your life. I personally know this to be a fact because this law has done just that for me. The law of supply is one of the greatest secrets of successful living that I have ever discovered. Considerable numbers of people to whom I have suggested this marvelous way of thinking and doing will enthusiastically endorse the positive assurance I give you here.

What is the law of supply? It is the operation of the principle of abundance spoken of by Jesus Christ when He said, "I have come that they may have life, and that they may have it more abundantly" (John 10:10). It is stated again in Luke 17:21, "The kingdom of God is within you," which is a reference to all the great values and blessings of life—hope, health, love, joy, and every good thing built into you by the Creator. According to the law of supply, your own good seeks to come to you and will continue to flow abundantly toward you if you do not block the flow by negative thought and action. When you become a true believer and are positive and outgoing in your faith, thinking your best, doing your best, and being your best, the law of generous supply starts working. Then God can activate your good, which He provides, and send it flowing unhindered to you.

My wife, Ruth, and I have practiced this principle since we were first married. We began married life with a minimum of financial support, but Ruth, a natural-born positive thinker and a woman of undiluted faith, always stoutly affirmed even in our times of dire circumstances that the Lord would provide. If we did our part and tried to help people as much as we were capable and trusted and had faith, we would, she declared, be taken care of and always would be given strength to carry on. In

developing this philosophy, sh. ....
one of the subtlest of all laws, the law of supp...

We had been practicing this principle for twenty years before we heard a name put to it. Our son John had been entered as a student in Deerfield Academy in Massachusetts, and there we came to know Dr. Frank Boyden, one of the greatest head-masters America has ever had and certainly one of its outstanding schoolmen. Frank was spiritually and intellectually wise, and he was a true positive thinker. As he showed us over the magnificent cam-pus with its splendid buildings and superb equip-ment, I marveled, since I knew he had built this school from a minuscule beginning.

"How did you ever do it?" I asked.

He smiled and said, "I'm sure the bank wrote me off a good many times, but I felt that I was doing God's work in helping boys to become good and successful men. And since the heavenly Father had, I felt, called me to do this job, I knew He would never let me fail. So the funds always came and they keep on coming. I was on the receiving end of God's law of supply. When you give all you can, God will give abundantly in return," he concluded.

As Frank spoke, I found myself thinking of that significant reference to this law of supply in Malachi 3:10:

> "Bring all the tithes into the storehouse,
>   That there may be food in My house,
>   And prove Me now in this,"
> Says the LORD of hosts,

"If I will not open for you the windows
　　of heaven
And pour out for you such blessing
That there will not be room enough to
　　receive it."

Ruth and I had been tithers, even when we had practically no material things. And we had been recipients of God's boundless blessings. So in this conversation with Frank Boyden, I knew that we had been working with a basic law of prosperity. As we drove away from Deerfield that day, Ruth said, almost with awe, "The law of supply—why, that is what we have been practicing all our lives. That's our big secret of living."

"It's yours, honey," I said. "I learned it from you, and you learned it from the Lord."

Now, years later, we are still tithers, giving not 10 percent but often 20 and even 30 percent. I would never even consider modifying this practice, for I believe it to be the activation of the continuous law of supply. And when to financial giving one adds the giving of love and help to people, then good returns in even more abundance. The original meaning of the word *abundant* meant "to rise up in waves"; your good rises up in the full flow of divine generosity.

When things are not going well and you are striving for the answer to your problem of how to make them go better, I suggest that you give thought to this basic way of turning adversity around, the practice of the law of supply. The truth is that God the Father wants you to prosper. The first psalm says so:

> Blessed is the man
>   Who walks not in the counsel of the
>   ungodly. . . .
> He shall be like a tree
>   Planted by the rivers of water,
>   That brings forth its fruit in its season,
>   Whose leaf also shall not wither;
> And whatever he does shall prosper (vv. 1,3).

The Bible, in which we have the most perfect use of language to describe the greatest things, finds it difficult to describe the riches almighty God desires to give us. In 1 Corinthians 2:9 is stated, "Eye has not seen, nor ear heard, / Nor have entered into the heart of man / The things which God has prepared for those who love Him." The Creator of all scientific law also created the law of supply to deliver marvelous values to us out of His boundless supply. So it would seem that when things are not going well, we are out of creative contact. Therefore to make things go better, we have only to establish a more perfect connection with the abundant flow of good.

The wise Dr. Samuel Johnson once declared, "It's worth at least a thousand pounds a year to have a bright point of view." I think it is worth much more than that since gloomy-thinking negativism is so contrary to prosperity as to actually chase it away. Prosperity turns away from the doubt-filled mind.

Remember, doubts tend to produce doubtful results. "All things work together for good to those who love God," the Bible tells us in Romans 8:28. Every morning remind yourself that since all things are working together for good for you, doors will open, new opportunities will come, and things will go better for you. By lifting anxiety from your mind, this powerful, sound belief will stimulate creative thinking and shift circumstances in your favor. But you must believe this, really believe it, to activate your mental process accordingly. Continue to believe and you will experience perhaps the best of all descriptions of spiritually induced prosperity, the words of the old hymn, "There shall be showers of blessing sent from the Saviour above."

Never say that blessings are scarce or even that money is scarce; the very assertion can scare both away from you. The only difference between the words *scare* and *scarce* is the one little letter *c*. Do not say that times are hard, for as Charles Fillmore wisely asserted, "The very words will tighten your purse strings until omnipotence itself cannot slip a dime into it. Fill every nook and corner of your mind with the word *plenty, plenty, plenty*." Every day at morning, noon, and night affirm aloud "plenty, plenty, plenty" and then, again aloud, say "opportunity, opportunity, opportunity." Meanwhile, image, visualize, picture plenty and opportunity. Empty out your negative, gloomy thoughts that scare away prosperity, and fill your mind with these bright, optimistic, positive thoughts that attract and draw the good that a generous God wants to send your way through your creative thinking.

Never think or talk lack because the grave danger is to actualize lack. When you send out such negative thoughts, the result is to activate the world around you negatively. Remember that like attracts like. When you constantly send out negative thoughts, you strongly tend to draw back negative results. You should never entertain or express an idea unless you wish it to take form in your life. In the Old Testament is the promise, "You will also declare a thing, / And it will be established for you" (Job 22:28).

When you say, "I am poor," you are in effect declaring poverty. Your word is the expression of your mental image. It is vital when things are not going well to avoid holding a failure image. The mind, which always works to serve you, will grasp at it to establish failure as a fact. Instead you must compel better things to develop by thought discipline. Thoughts and words can speak life or death to your future. Remember, lack thoughts and lack words tend to produce lack as fact. Remember also the truth that prosperity thoughts and prosperity words move you in the direction of prosperity and increased success, because you tend to become what you think and affirm, pray and visualize.

The principles outlined in this book are demonstrable truths, evidenced in the experiences of many persons. People who believed in these principles and put them to work in real situations have found that they definitely cause things to go better, much better. They discovered the proof of the pudding, so to speak.

If you *can* only believe! If you *will* only believe! Then nothing, *nothing,* will be impossible for you! That is the truth and the gospel, and it is wonderful. It's the good news.

I visited an industrial organization that had signs all over the factory and the offices adjoining the plant. On each sign was the one word *Think*. That was all the sign said. Curious, I asked the head of the firm about the signs. He explained that they were his idea. The purpose was to stimulate employees to come up with new ideas to add to the company's total efficiency. But beyond that purpose, the company president was enthusiastic about developing people who worked for him, "and," he said, "if you can get a person into the habit of really doing some hard, constructive thinking about his or her job, that individual is destined to advance in responsibility and income."

He told me about a number of people who had thought up innovative procedures. Some were just small things, but others were revolutionary. The result was a company spirit of participation that benefited the total organization. "But in a few cases, getting people to think revolutionized the life and career of employees who, while they would have done satisfactory routine jobs, would otherwise never have gone up the ladder.

Any job will respond to sound thinking; out of thinking come ideas that make things go better.

And when the thinking you do is positive, you have a double-pronged tool for achieving improvement.

If you are convinced of the truth and practical workability of what you are reading here, the smart thing to do is to act now on your conviction. You may get an immediate result or it may be delayed. But in either case, go with your faith, hang in there with it. Keep on believing, believing, believing. And keep thinking. Keep action going and you will enjoy improved circumstances.

In the home of Commander and Mrs. Geoffrey Kitson in Bermuda, I noticed a framed quotation on a wall. It read, "Everyone has inside himself—what shall I call it—a piece of good news." What is that good news? Well, it could be that you and I are greater than anything that can ever happen to us. Or it could be that we have it in us to overcome anything that would ever get us down. Certainly those words can mean that we have what it takes to improve a present situation and make things go better. There is an achiever, a winner, in every one of us, and that is good news.

Thomas A. Edison also had a framed sign on his studio wall: "There is a better way of doing it. Find it." You can do that better job and get things going better all the while. As I think along this line and reflect upon the remarkable men and women I have known who improved their situation by improving themselves, I always recall an unforgettable verse from the book of Job: "If you return to the Almighty, you will be built up" (22:23). Being built up, you will be bigger than any discouragement, any setback, any failure.

That is a valid piece of good news within you, one for which you can be grateful. You and I can be built up so as to tower above our failures and, despite all difficulties, make things better than ever before. We can get into the habit of expecting and experiencing self-improvement and the habit of turning a current condition into a better state.

After I finished a speech in a city auditorium, a man came backstage who really was in a miserable state of mind. He was young, perhaps thirty years of age, and he told me he faced a hopeless situation. He added glumly that I was "his last hope." How could he improve his situation, rebuild his shattered career? I stated quickly that I was not his last hope—he and God were—but I told him that I would be glad to help in any way possible.

I let him talk for a while, ventilating his depressed thoughts. I noticed that he was about six two or three, but he was slumped down, bent over, his head on his chest while he told me all the reasons why he could not meet his situation, to say nothing of improving it. Suddenly with seeming irrelevance, I asked, "Will you do me a favor, my friend?"

Surprised he said hesitantly, "What do you want me to do?"

"Stand up, stand up as tall as you can." He complied, but he stood with his shoulders slumped. I asked, "How tall are you anyway?"

"Six feet two when I stand up straight."

"Well, please stand up straight now. Make your height your total six two. I'd like to see it. Nature has been good to you to give you height like that." Thus prodded he struggled to achieve his full height. "Look at that," I exclaimed in admiration, "six two! What a man!"

He still looked at me in some surprise, but it was interesting to see him straighten up, trying to reach even higher. "Doesn't that feel much better than when you were lopped over to about five five a few minutes ago?" I asked.

"Yes, I do feel better, funny but I really do."

So I gave him a formula. "Here is how you can meet your situation and turn it around. Do the following three things. First, several times each day stand tall, reaching for the sky with the crown of your head. Lift your head up as far as it will go, and try to reach for infinity. When God created you, He made you on your two feet to stand tall. And He gave you a head, and the head is supposed to be carried high. When a person maintains this erect stature, whatever his height, he has a commanding power over life and circumstances. So stand tall.

"Second, think tall. Think big thoughts, victorious thoughts. Think winning thoughts. Stand tall mentally. You have been giving me a desultory, gloomy mass of negative, unhappy, frustrated, defeated thoughts. Now that you are standing tall physically, also stand tall mentally. Positively practice positive affirmation." And the first such affirmation I gave him was "It can be done and I can do it!" I said, "Please say that."

"You mean out loud?"

"Certainly! Let's say it together. It can be done and I can do it." So I had him there standing tall, thinking tall, and affirming that he had a stature physically and mentally that towered over his so-called failure situation.

"Third," I suggested, "stand tall spiritually. Think of the greatness of God. Think of yourself as an undefeatable child of God. Ten times every day repeat aloud one of the greatest affirmative statements of faith: 'I can do all things through Christ who strengthens me.' And make a start by doing that now." By this time he was getting the message and actually getting into the spirit of overcoming.

Almost word for word, this is the conversation we had in about ten minutes. I could already see him changing into a victorious, winning person as a new positive attitude began taking hold. "Okay, Dr. Peale, okay. Thanks a lot. I know I can improve my situation, and with the Lord's help I will do it." So saying, he walked out into the night.

This man actually returned to the Almighty and became built up. Of course he had his moments of uncertainty, even slumping down occasionally, but he made the grade because he was changed in his thoughts. His attitude was revamped. He found the good news that was built into him. In the last analysis, nobody ever changes a situation unless he gets changed himself. Every outside situation is a reflection of the internal condition. Get changed on the inside, become a changed person, become a new man or woman, and you can handle and improve any situation. And that is a fact, a big, certain fact.

So I end this chapter as it began: shoot for the moon. Even if you miss it, you will land among the stars.

We are now ready to talk about today, this wonderful, opportunity-packed today. In the next chapter I have a winning slogan for you: "Today is yours, seize it!"

6.

Today Is Yours, Seize It

POSITIVE THINKERS get positive results because they appreciate the inestimable value of a day, this day, not the next day, but *this* day, and every day. Today offers at least sixteen waking hours that may be crammed full of opportunity, joy, excitement, achievement. The positive thinker knows that today was made for him and for everyone who will go for it positively. Today is his, so he makes it a marvelous creative experience. The positive thinker's optimistic attitude toward today and every succeeding day strongly tends to make every day a great day. It becomes what he visualizes it to be.

Every morning for many years, the first thing upon rising, I have quoted a dynamic, upbeat statement that I found in the most creative of all books. It has done wonders for me. Sometimes I repeat it aloud, sometimes I think it quietly, but always it vitalizes my attitude and activates my faith. It really gets me going at full power for the day. Moreover, through speeches and books and by one-on-one contact, I probably have persuaded thousands to adopt the same get-up-in-the-morning habit. There is no doubt whatsoever that it effectively conditions the day. Here are those life-packed, inspiration-filled, get-going words that help me every morning, rain or shine, to take my day and do something with it: "This is the day which the LORD has made;/ We will rejoice and be glad in it" (Ps. 118:24).

And every now and then my wife will say at breakfast, "Let's have a good day today," and we proceed to do just that. A positive attitude toward every day works out so well that I am motivated to write this chapter, "Today Is Yours." You must seize it because it is fleeting, only twenty-four hours that are soon gone by. If you live to be eighty years of age, you will have only 29,200 days. Each of them, therefore, is a precious fragment of a gift called time, your time. It only makes sense to use every day well. Today is yours. Use it well.

The place was Korea. The hour 1:00 A.M. The temperature was below zero. It was so cold that bare fingers stuck to metal. A big burly marine was leaning against a tank and eating cold beans out of a can with a penknife. A newspaper correspondent watching him, aware that a big battle was building up, asked a philosophical question. "Look, if I were God and could give you anything, what would you ask for?"

The marine dug out another mouthful of beans with his knife, thought the question over, and then said, "I would ask for today."

I believe we all should. Fortunately, we have today. What are we going to do with it? The answer is easy. We are going to carry on working toward our goals. And despite any reverses, setbacks, or difficulties that may come, we are going to be achievers because we are positive thinkers. We are going to reach those goals and have a rare good time in the process. We are going to have the immense satisfaction of being winners.

Positive thinkers get positive results because they love life, see good days, get in there, and give themselves to their days, every one of them, with enthusiasm. In turn, their days will come back to them. It is a fact that if people love life, life will love them back. And it will joyously give back to them in proportion as they give to it.

My wife, Ruth, and I were out in that great country of Alberta, Canada, where the vast prairies surge up against the mighty Rocky Mountains. I had given a speech in Calgary. Early the next morning, Ruth and I went to the airport. The temperature registered twenty-five degrees, the air was crisp and pollution free. The sky was a clear blue, not a cloud in sight. It was a beautiful, cold but sunny November day.

We had over an hour before departure, and feeling alive to our fingertips, we decided to take a brisk walk. Soon we were out of the airport grounds onto the prairie itself. Then we turned about, and there in clear view were the Rockies in breathtaking panorama. They were covered with snow, sparkling like thousands of diamonds in the sunlight. We counted sixty-two snowclad peaks. "Isn't this terrific!" I exclaimed. Ruth's eyes were bright with the delight of the morning and the beauty about us.

Later when our plane took off over a low hill, there, spread out before us from north to south against an azure sky, were many more white peaks. I was so moved by it all that I said, "You know, honey, I love this. I really love it all. I don't want to leave this incredible, wonderful world. I want to live a long time. This is so fascinating, so very great."

Always of a practical turn of mind, Ruth responded, "Well, if you practice that positive thinking you talk about, you will live a long time. You'll have lots of days yet to come. Tell you what. Let's take today and every succeeding day and fill each one full of the beauty and romance and joy of the life God gives us."

So today is yours, dear friend. Seize it! Grab it! Love it! Live it!

Someone might glumly object that all this sounds like a lot of moonlight-and-roses stuff. Such a person might ask, "But what about the tough breaks that come along? How are you going to equate all the dark, even tragic days, with this beautiful talk about good days every day?"

Well, no one has actually raised this question with me, but I have raised it with myself. Having had quite a lot of so-called tough breaks of my own, I long ago faced up to the necessity of working out a positive philosophy about tough breaks in life's total experience. Actually the problem is not so much what happens to you as what you think and do about what happens to you, because a lot of harsh things can come to you.

This one day, whatever it may bring, belongs to you and to me to handle so that the best results can be obtained from what may seem the worst. The secret, of course, is to inject hope into despair and faith into defeat.

The late Casey Stengel, famed manager of the New York Yankees, had the idea in simple form. It was said that defeat did not awe Casey because in every defeat he was always looking for victory. It seems that defeat only motivated him to win more victories. The tough breaks that made some days difficult impelled him to turn the breaks his way the next day.

Personally I have found a lot of help in the truth that to every disadvantage there is a corresponding advantage. And it has always helped me when the going was hard to recall an old proverb, "The hammer shatters glass but forges steel." If you are made of good stuff, then the tough breaks will not break you but will make you hard like steel. And you will think of bad days as good days because of your attitude.

Captain Max Cleland was a vigorous young man on that morning back in 1968 in Vietnam. But before night came, his strong body was wrecked—an exploding grenade took off both his legs and his left arm. Then followed months of physical suffering and mental agony and adjustment. It seemed unlikely that any days ahead could be his to seize and do with creatively. But Cleland had strong, tough faith. He had been noted for a ringing laugh and an infectious smile, and he kept that laugh. Of course he had times of despair and days when it seemed he could never make it.

But Max Cleland went home to Georgia to serve two terms as a state senator. Then he ran for lieutenant governor. When he lost, he was crushed, and depression seized him once again. It was then that something happened to restore good days to Max. Driving in the rain to Washington, D.C., to take a Senate staff position, he suddenly realized, as he described it, "I could go no further by myself. On that rain-swept highway I threw myself at the Lord's feet and cried out, 'God forgive me and help me.' When I reached out, He came to me.

"Since then I really have become stronger at the broken places. And today I find more meaning, more purpose, and more joy in life than I ever thought possible." Despite being able to move only by wheelchair, Max Cleland is in the midst of an illustrious career. President Carter appointed him administrator of the Veterans Administration, the largest department of the federal government, in which capacity he served with distinction. Later he was elected Georgia secretary of state by a large majority. I have watched admiringly as he fascinated large audiences by his matchless speaking ability, persuasive sincerity, and upbeat positive faith. If I were to name the ten happiest persons of my acquaintance, "handicapped" Max Cleland would be on that list.

How did he become a good-day expert, a genius in victorious living? He cites three principles: (1) Strive for acceptance of the problem. He prayed the famous prayer, "God grant me the serenity to accept the things I cannot change." (2) Find another door that opens, because when one door closes, another swings wide open. Don't look so closely at the closed door that you miss the one that is opening. "I still had my mind and one strong arm to propel a wheelchair." (3) Let God help you.

That God is helping him over the rough spots, keeping him happy all the way, is obvious to all who know him. Despite the horrendous things that happened to him, Max Cleland did not fold up in defeat. He had the tremendous positive spirit to know that today was still his; he grabbed it and made something extraordinary of it.

Ann Person was flat on her back in the hospital. Her husband, Herb, was ill. The family was practically destitute. The future looked grim indeed. But Ann wasn't defeated because she could do two basic things, think and pray. As long as one can do that, there is always hope. And an idea focused in Ann's mind that led to a spectacular success. But let her tell her story in her own words as she related it in part to *Guideposts* magazine.

In October 1965, I lay flat on my back in the tuberculosis ward of Oregon's state hospital. Bleakly, I stared up at the ceiling. With my illness had come depression. I realized that I didn't have much to show for the past 40 years. I had frittered my adulthood away; dabbling in everything, but committing myself to nothing.

As a child as I stitched my first doll's dress I was sure I would grow up to be a world-famous fashion designer. And for many years I pursued my goal.

But somewhere along the way my enthusiasm waned and my dream of a glamorous career faded. My life, once full of vitality and purpose, became lackluster and drab. Even my health began to decline.

Never had I felt so alone and empty—and scared—as in that hospital bed. "Lord," I whispered, "I'm scared. If You'll just get me out of this, I promise I'll do something worthwhile with my life. I know I can't do it without Your help. You've got to show me the way. But give me a chance."

In the silence that followed there was an indescribable feeling of comfort. I slept peacefully, secure in knowing that by turning the situation over to God, I had done everything I could.

I felt rejuvenated—excited, somehow, about what the future held in store. Remembering my prayer, I felt confident that I would find my niche soon.

It was in my sewing classes that I felt most strongly my old enthusiasm bubbling up inside me. Students would often tell me they'd never felt so motivated.

One day, an appreciative student sent me a

huge carton of knit fabric remnants from a mill-end factory outlet. Knits, at that time, were new on the market and virtually unknown to most home seamstresses. Those who were familiar with the fabric considered it difficult, if not impossible, to work with. Countless times, I'd heard friends complain how knits bagged, sagged and raveled hopelessly.

Still, the riot of colors and textures peeking out from that box were irresistible. "Try me," they seemed to say. I pulled out a large kelly green remnant, sat down at my machine and began experimenting. Once I started, it became difficult to stop. I felt a tingle of excitement as one discovery followed another.

The best results, I learned, came from using big stitches, *stretching* the fabric as I sewed. Word spread, and before I knew it, my classes were devoted entirely to my new "stretch and sew" method with knits. Came a phone call from a woman in a small town. Would I be willing to drive down and demonstrate my techniques to a few of her friends? *Do it,* a small voice urged, and I accepted. When I arrived 70 ladies were waiting. And that one session initiated a chain of classes that kept me on a 500-mile, statewide weekly circuit for the remainder of the year.

I was on fire with an enthusiasm for my work and life that I hadn't known since childhood, and I knew without a doubt that the source of this vitality was God. For the first time in my life, I was finally doing what I *should* be doing. I had found my niche.

We copyrighted the name "Stretch and Sew," and I began training and licensing others to conduct the "Basic Eight" series of lessons. Six months later we opened the first Stretch and Sew Center, where classes were held and exclusive Stretch and Sew knit fabrics, notions, and patterns were sold. I put together one of the first books ever published about sewing with knits, featuring easy-to-understand language. Incredibly, the book *Stretch & Sew* sold more than a million copies, and its success led to a five-year national television series called *Sewing with Ann Person*.

Herb came up with the idea of a franchised Stretch and Sew Sewing Center system. Today there are 239 such centers throughout the U.S. and Canada, where millions of women are learning the Stretch and Sew way. Recently, at the close of a workshop in a midwestern city, a small woman came up to me.

"Ann," she said quietly, "I'm a widow. For years after my husband died, I was alone and desperate. I didn't know who I was; I didn't want to live. I signed up for your classes just to pass the time—but through them I gained a sense of self-worth I never had. I learned how to set goals and make decisions. I made friends. It was just the boost I needed, and I just want to thank you . . . and thank God."*

The more we read such success stories, the more we should realize that we can do things ourselves.

*Exerpted with permission from Guideposts Magazine. Copyright © 1981 by Guideposts Associates, Inc., Carmel, New York 10512.

Amazing creative power may be lying unused within you. Never allow potential in your personality to languish. Do not let it wither and die. All you need to do is stop thinking negatively and start taking a positive attitude about yourself. Cultivate belief. Make yourself believe in yourself and in your hidden talents and ability. Think and think and think some more and, to thinking, add prayer; these two procedures are miracle workers. And to both of them, add courage and fortitude. Such action can find and release talents you never realized you possessed. Then will come a day, a big wonderful day, when you will clearly picture who you are and what you can be. Then you will exclaim, "Today is mine!" You will seize it and that will be the day. Ann Person did not know that she had a creative enterprise locked within her, but by the process I've outlined here she found that she did.

I was riding one night with a man taking me to a speaking engagement. As we passed a farmhouse, he said, "Funny thing happened there. A man lived in that house who let it run down until it was almost in ruins. And he seemed run-down also. He dressed in such a shabby manner that he appeared extremely poverty-stricken. He lived from hand to mouth. Then he died, and shortly afterward the county put a feeder road through his farm. In excavating for the road, workers unearthed several milk cans. They were crammed with money, about $200,000 in bills—fives, tens, twenties."

It was discovered that this "poor" man had at one time owned stock, but he had sold it and buried the cash in the milk cans. "Foolish, pathetic fellow," we say, but he was certainly no more foolish or pathetic than those of us who bury our talent under a mass of negative thinking and, as a result, live in a personality poverty. The positive person will see clearly the resources and opportunities available to him. He will make the most of every day and every situation. He will even see opportunity where none appears to exist and do something outstanding.

I was lucky enough never to be offered a job that was already succeeding. I think I was lucky because a job already at a high level has to be maintained there or upped still further. If the job is at low ebb, an individual can become successful by developing it and improving it. I was offered and I accepted four churches in my life as a minister, and each one was at the point of failure, even disintegration. In each case I had the opportunity to turn the situation around and bring the four churches to a successful condition.

I did not know it at the time, but this was the big good fortune of my professional life. In fact, I recommend taking on a position that is down in preference to one that is going well. In making the low one successful, you make yourself a success. Anyway, such was my opportunity, and each time I took a poor job, it proved to be the greatest chance to come my way.

How do some positive thinkers get powerful results when faced with difficult situations? I think of Dr. Raj Chopra, a successful educator who received an offer from a midwestern city board of education to become superintendent of their school district. A CBS "60 Minutes" television report on this particular school system had declared that students' test scores in that city were the worst in the state, that it was a failing school system, consisting of twenty-two elementary, five junior high, and two high schools. But, even knowing all this, Dr. Chopra went to see for himself whether this job might be a challenge for him. He is a positive thinker who likes to tackle difficult jobs.

What he encountered was a pretty negative situation. The hotel clerk recognized his name when he checked in and sardonically said, "Good luck. You'll need it." The clerk told him that demoralized teachers were fleeing to other jobs. As Dr. Chopra went about town talking to people, he sensed a generally depressed attitude toward the town, a poor self-image caused perhaps in part by the television report. Hardly anyone had anything good to say about the local schools, and some advised him not to take the job. "You'll only hurt yourself," they warned.

But Dr. Chopra met the one person who finally convinced him that he ought not to accept the job. The man was sitting on his front doorstep and drinking a can of beer. There was an elementary school next door. Dr. Chopra asked him what he thought about his community's schools. "The man stared at me for a moment," said Dr. Chopra, "lowered his can of beer, turned toward the school, and snapped, 'If that place was on fire, I wouldn't throw a bucket of water on it.'" That was the last straw, and Dr. Chopra couldn't get home fast enough.

At dinner in his home he described this depressing situation to his family, saying that there was no hope for the school system. The family was quiet for a moment; then his young son Dick spoke up, "But, Dad, what about your faith? You're always telling us how problems should be opportunities." The father knew that his son was right. So he reversed his decision and took the job.

He said of his experience:

My first priority was getting out into the school and visiting with students and teachers. One morning as I walked through a school hall, a teacher came toward me. I greeted her, "Good morning, Mrs. Jones."

"What's good about it?" she grumped.

"It's good because I have this opportunity to look at your beautiful face."

She looked a bit startled, but I continued.

"Mrs. Jones, the morning is good because both of us are looking forward to working with young people today. It's exciting to know that we are going to make this day better for them."

She stared at me dubiously.

"Well, isn't it a good morning?"

"Absolutely!" she laughed.

Enthusiasm is contagious; it's transmitted from one to another. But you can't generate it in others unless you have it yourself.

One way to become enthusiastic is to look for the plus sign. To make progress in any difficult situation, you have to start with what's right about it and build on that. When a hue and cry is raised that 20 percent of the students cannot read, I've found that first I have to tell parents that 80 percent of the students *can* read. After that we start talking about what to do with the other 20 percent. With any tough situation, the best hope is to start working on it from the positive side.

When I visited my first classroom in the run-down school system I was impressed by the inquisitive young faces I saw there. Were these the same children who had ranked so low on test scores? They didn't look any different from students I'd seen in other cities. In fact, they looked very intelligent to me. And I decided to tell them so.

"I want you all to know that I think you are among the brightest children I have met," I said, "I'm proud to be associated with you." As I told them how certain I felt that they would do exceedingly well in the coming year, I saw a look of expectancy brighten their faces.

In telling our teachers that we appreciated their skills, we also let them know we *expected* the best.

We always tried to impress upon our principals, supervisors and teachers the power that lies within each and every one of us to make a difference in other people's lives.

How did it all work out? Were the gloom-and-doom prophets right?

Student test scores soared to a new high, teacher morale was up, and parents were proud—so proud that they'd begun sponsoring an annual "Pride Week" with a big parade down Main Street honoring their school and community.

What made the difference? Simple principles of positive thinking, or "power principles" as I like to call them. No matter where you are, you can use positive attitudes. Here they are:

1. Be enthusiastic.
2. See the good.
3. Expect the best.
4. Learn that "I can make the difference."
5. Believe!

Dr. Chopra was subsequently called to be superintendent of one of the great school districts in the nation, the Shawnee school system in the Kansas City area.

There is an old saying, "One never knows what a day will bring forth." You have only one day at a time. No day is just another day, another routine twenty-four hours. This day, any day, may contain your golden opportunity, perhaps even the big opportunity of a lifetime. You may make a decision today that may affect the rest of your life. Be alert today because opportunity may come.

If you have missed opportunities, turn your thoughts to today. Acquire know-how from past experience but never bog down in postmortems. Appreciate the precious value inherent in this one new day. Visualize other and greater opportunities in store for you. Above all, never minimize the opportunity that may involve a tough situation. Gold comes laced in rocks. So does the chance of a lifetime. As a positive thinker, you will get powerful results if you believe that this day is yours and seize it.

It has been my privilege to speak at many positive thinking rallies or, as such meetings are sometimes called, success motivation conventions. These usually attract large crowds numbering from five to ten thousand, mostly young men and women who come to listen to several speakers for the avowed purpose of doing more with their lives. Sometimes employers, wanting to encourage their employees, buy blocks of tickets for these meetings.

All speakers can no doubt tell of people whose lives were turned around in such meetings. There is something about a big meeting, a kind of creative atmosphere, that seems made for miracles of personality change. At any rate, time and again men and women have told me that "something happened" to them and they were never the same again. They became focused; they found themselves discovering powers they never knew they had. Thus it was that on one particular day they became new persons, surprising even themselves, by the hitherto unknown potential they demonstrated. They found that this was their day, and they seized it and went on to outstanding success.

One night I was speaking with two men in Chattanooga at a motivational rally. Being the last speaker of the evening, I went from backstage to almost the last row of the balcony to watch the effect of my fellow speakers on the huge crowd. An obliging young man moved over to give me the aisle seat, and before the rally began we had a pleasant conversation. But he did not know who I was.

Shortly after the first speaker began, I noted that my fellow seatmate was nodding and presently was sound asleep. He roused a bit when some humorous remark caused general laughter, but then he quietly sank back into sleep. The applause at the conclusion of the talk awakened him. "Pretty good, wasn't he?" observed my friend.

How would you know? I thought of saying but didn't.

But I did say, "This next speaker is one of the best. He found the success secret for himself and tells about it. I know of many fellows who were not getting anywhere but who listened to this speaker and were literally blasted out of sleepy indifference. They became balls of fire and terrific successes."

"I'll sure listen," he said. To my surprise, he did listen. The speaker seemed to get this sleepy fellow with his first remark. "Listen, whoever you are, wherever you are. This can be your great day. You can be changed in the next few minutes. Your great unreleased potential can become activated. So listen, listen, listen," he thundered. "Destiny is calling you now, this day."

The young fellow didn't slump into sleep. He sat up straight, leaned forward, and drank in every word. He was fascinated, sitting spellbound for the next forty minutes. At the conclusion of the speech he muttered, "I've got to touch him, shake his hand. He got to me, he got to me." With a word of apology he brushed past me and rushed down the balcony steps toward the stage.

I never saw him again, but later I asked the speaker whether a young man six feet plus with blond hair might have grabbed his hand with more than the usual zeal. "He did indeed, and he said something had happened to him. He declared that he would never forget this day."

Several years later I asked this same speaker if he remembered this incident. "Oh, yes," he replied, "and that fellow is one of my greatest examples of how, under the influence of one minute of motivation that really connects, a person can find his day, seize it, and never be the same old failure anymore."

We can never know in advance when our big moment will come. However, if we believe that our purpose in this world is not yet fulfilled, our day will come. And then we must surely seize it and go on from there to achieve our destiny.

That fulfillment of your life can begin any day. It can get into motion now, today, as you read this book. If the impulse is sufficiently strong, the motivation definite, a person drawing deeply upon the basic potential locked within can produce astounding results.

Recently I dedicated a chapel in a large industrial plant in Philadelphia. On the day of dedication the exquisite chapel was filled by a large gathering of the leaders of the city to honor the company's founder, Michael Cardone. He and his wife overcame poverty to create the huge factory now employing many hundreds of persons.

These capable people had their day when the idea came to them to redo or reclaim old automobile parts and accessories, from windshield wipers to motors. Many persons would not have seen the astonishing extent to which this idea could be developed, and few would have undertaken it. But the Cardones had faith, they believed that the Lord was guiding them. They seized the day and went with the idea of making new windshield wipers and new motors out of old ones. Today Cardone Industries, a complex of buildings with a chapel for the worship of God at the center, is one of the outstanding examples of the American system of free enterprise. And it is an example of two believing people who lived by the truth that today is yours, seize it.

Of course the positive approach to life has an enemy, a sly, devious enemy called discouragement. Discouragement lurks nearby to get in its depressing work whenever possible, but there is a weapon that can effectively destroy discouragement. I will tell about it in Chapter 7, "The Positive Thinker Wins Over Discouragement."

7.

The Positive Thinker Wins Over Discouragement

DOES THE positive thinker ever get discouraged? Of course. He is a human being, subject to the rise and fall of moods. But the positive thinker does not remain discouraged because he learns how to deal with this feeling.

Spirit is variable, a mixture of light and dark, up and down, joy and gloom, a rhythmic variation of levels. It is easier to let the down cycle take over than to maintain the up cycle of spirit. The latter requires desire, will, and effort with a pattern of uplifting thoughts.

Hence as a positive thinker, you must take authority over the rhythmic mood cycle. When it goes down, ride with it, but mentally make your thought control bring it upward quickly. As a result, while discouragement comes at intervals, you must not give in to it or settle down in it. Turn on your mental lifting power and rise up over the discouraging mood. The positive thinker wins over discouragement.

It is not necessarily an easy process to become proficient in mastering discouragement. It requires know-how. You have to understand the causes of discouraged attitudes. Once you become knowledgeable about the variableness of spirit, the next step is to develop insight into the law of spirit and understand mood cycles.

Then you must study workable and effective techniques of spirit acceleration. You must investigate and experiment with various mood lifters until you find procedures that work for you and are adaptable to your particular personality characteristics.

In this chapter I will suggest some practical techniques for overcoming discouragement that have been helpful to me and to many others. You might try them separately or in combination. By experimentation you can arrive at an antidiscouragement methodology that will give you a perpetual mastery over the dark moods that attack your positive, enthusiastic spirit.

Here is antidiscouragement suggestion number one: *you must really want to overcome discouragement*. It is as simple as that. You must truly want to be healed of the discouragement tendency. But you may ask, "How can anyone not want to be rid of the habit of being discouraged? How can anyone is his right mind not go all out to banish discouragement from his life?" The answer is that perhaps few of us are always in our so-called right mind. That is to say, we have a certain amount of the illogical within us. All of us are a mixture of reason and unreason. We do not always think straight.

We can use discouragement to cover up failure and to rationalize our inability to make it successfully. So we can tell ourselves defensively, "You see, I always knew I didn't have it in me." And then we can retire to the dark shadows in the mind and console ourselves. In a sense, discouragement is a kind of retreat where we can escape reality and soothe ourselves in self-pity. Accordingly, the semi-defeated person, the halfway negative thinker, does not quite want to let go of the crutch of discouragement, because without it he has lost his mechanism for escape from a competitive world.

Moreover, there is in all persons, though in some more than in others, what may be called a masochistic or self-punishment streak. Such people seem to have a need for self-flagellation, not in any dramatic form, but in the milder form of holding dark, gloomy thoughts. They get a certain satisfaction from retiring into gloom and depression. Granted, this reaction verges on the abnormal, but not everyone is completely normal in all reactions. Yet it is possible to be normal, which is one of the objectives of positive thinking.

Take charge of your thoughts. You can do what you will with them. When you want to get through with discouragement, when with all—completely all—of your mind and all of your heart and all of your soul you definitely, absolutely want to cast it out of your life forever, then you are on the victory trail. When you want to badly enough, you can stand up to your thoughts and direct them instead of letting them push you around.

A good example is Merton DeForrest, who passed over the river not so long ago with all his flags flying and bugles blowing. He had a long fight with discouragement and often retreated glumly into dark, gloomy thoughts to nurse his mental wounds. But finally he became fed up with his pathetic life-style. He had a powerful spiritual experience, which completely changed him deep in his nature. He read *The Power of Positive Thinking*, and what is more important, he practiced it. One day he faced his discouragement tendency. Mentally he took it in hand and authoritatively declared, "Listen, you, get this straight. I'm in charge of my life. Not you. So you get out and stay out."

Seems strange to talk thus to an attitude, but it is not strange. It is realistic. When you become assertive and mean it, a destructive attitude will inevitably back down, and if you continue to assume control, the attitude will eventually give up, as DeForrest discovered.

Sounds like bravado? Whistling in the dark? Not at all. It is the magnificent assertiveness and authority of a sovereign individual, a child of God. It is the power of great personality in action. Remember what the Bible says about dominion? "Then God said, 'Let Us make man in Our image, according to Our likeness; let them have dominion. . . . So God created man in His own image; in the image of God He created him; male and female He created them. Then God blessed them, and God said to them, . . . 'have dominion' " (Gen. 1:26–28). That is what you are to do—take dominion. Take charge of your thoughts. Master the dark ones. Put your positive thoughts in charge. Take control of your life as God said you could. That is antidiscouragement suggestion number one.

A second technique is to *use silence* as I described in a plan I put in a thirty-four-page pocket-sized booklet *10 Minutes a Day to a Better Way*. It has been read and practiced by over one million people. (If you would like a copy of the booklet, write to the Foundation for Christian Living, P.O. Box FCL, Pawling, New York, 12564, and say you read about it in this book. They will be glad to send you a free copy.) The following is the outline of this plan and its application to the problem of discouragement.

The plan is to spend ten minutes every day in carefully selected thought procedures. A successful outcome will depend upon the regularity with which this routine is followed. Doing it for one day, two days, three days and then skipping a day or more will nullify the values that constant regularity of the ten-minute period brings.

Some have their ten-minute period in the early morning; others after breakfast; and still others at varying times during the day or evening. Being rigid about this practice is not recommended, but at some time within every twenty-four hours, the ten-minute period should be observed. If the plan is followed regularly, beneficial results will soon become apparent.

All of us, because of circumstances, think we have to let some things pass. But the person who seriously wants a better way must establish the rule of never letting a day go by without observing the ten-minute period.

Go into a room, close the door, and sit quietly. If the telephone rings, do not answer it. The same with the doorbell. Let nothing interfere with the spiritual, profoundly creative silence you will experience in the next ten minutes. Remember the wise words of Thomas Carlyle, "Silence is the element in which great things fashion themselves together." Scrupulously observe the silence.

Turn your mind to thoughts of God. Think only about Him for five minutes. Picture Him as a wise, kindly, loving Father. Say these words:

> "Silence. Silence.
> Heavenly Father.
> Kindly Father.
> My Father."

See Him as just that.
Then say:

> "The great God,
> the loving God,
> the protecting God."

Then add:

"Jesus Christ,
my Lord and Savior,
is helping me now."

If you do this as directed, you will be enveloped by a sense of peace.

For the second five minutes, image yourself as dropping discouragement into the eternal quietness, the everlasting silence, the great hands of God. Let go of it. See God taking it into His big hands. Let God handle it. As you do this, your mind is swept clean of dark shadows. Light fills every crevice of your mind. You are now able to think more clearly. Ideas by which you can successfully handle discouragement will emerge into consciousness.

As a young man, I was in a period of discouragement. I was crossing the Atlantic at the end of a vacation. Being unable to sleep, I dressed and went up on the top deck. It was totally dark. I stood watching as the darkness turned into gray and there were shadows everywhere. Then a faint glow of pink appeared on the eastern horizon. A sliver of the rising sun projected upward. Long shafts of light cut across the waters.

At this point a miracle happened. The great round sun seemed to leap out of the sea and burst forth in all its glory. Then I saw something I have never forgotten. The shadows, lurking in every nook and corner, started to run. Like mice, they scampered across the deck, seeming to jump into the sea, leaving the white ship without a shadow as it sailed serenely across the blue waters of the Atlantic. Suddenly my discouragement was gone.

When discouragement really begins to dominate, the positive thinker employs a third method for getting out from under its effects. *Have someone listen.* That helps get you back into a normal attitude.

I recall one day when my secretary came into my office to tell me that a woman demanded to see me.

"Has she an appointment and who is she?" I asked.

"No appointment and I do not know who she is beyond her name. She states that she was walking on the avenue and noticed your name on the sign board. She says she is a positive thinker in a bit of trouble, and she believes you can help her."

"Well, okay. Show her in. I'll talk to her."

The woman was businesslike. "Thank you for seeing me without an appointment. I'll state my business briefly. Then you can advise me, and I will get out of your hair and be on my way." Trouble came through despite her assumed jauntiness.

She then proceeded to talk without interruption. She had been studying to make a positive thinker of herself, but she said, "A lot of troubles and difficulties ganged up on me. Try as I can, discouragement has all but knocked out my positive attitude." She expressed her belief that if she could get on top of the discouraged feeling she "could get back on track and handle things."

"Empty it all out," I said. "I'm here to help you, so go ahead and talk. Ventilate the discouragement. I'll listen; and when you finish, I will come up with whatever I think might be helpful." So she went on steadily pouring out her troubles, not repeating them as some disorganized thinkers do, but in an orderly sequence of thought. Obviously she was a thinker, and I judged she had a rather important job.

After talking steadily for thirty minutes, she suddenly looked at her watch. "Oh, I have taken far too much of your time. Please forgive me. You have helped me a lot. I'll not forget your kindness to a total stranger." Then she departed my office as quickly as she had entered it. She left me wondering exactly what I had done for her. Then I realized I had helped by listening, and she had helped herself by emptying her mind.

When discouragement piles up, threatening to crush your spirit and frustrate your positive attitude, go to some understanding person who will listen creatively. Completely empty out the mass of accumulated dark and dismal thoughts. The mind, if it is to function well, must never be overburdened by negative thoughts, discouragement included.

Years later, when I was speaking at a motivational rally, a woman came along in a line of people waiting to speak to me following the talk, and she referred to this incident. "You helped me through a crisis that day," she said, "and thank God I've been on top ever since." That is what we are "in business" to do, to help people get on top and stay there.

Of course, it is not to be expected that the simple act of listening can always drain off discouragement as effectively as in this instance. But, that it did happen in this circumstance shows the validity of the mind-emptying process.

Let me give you a practical three-point formula

for getting rid of depression and discouragement:
(1) pray it out, (2) talk it out, and (3) think it out.
Ventilate it by praying to the great God who listens
and understands. Talk to some person who will, in
His name, listen and understand. Finally, use your
own reason, your own rationality, and think it out.
The secret is to talk out the problem to God, to
another person, and to yourself. Such a mental
and spiritual process of eliminating discouraging
thoughts, if continued rationally and not emotionally, has a powerful, curative effect.

A friend, whom I shall call Harold, had a series of
adversities, one after another, enough to take the
life out of just about anyone. But this man had a
strong faith and stood up admirably under the on-
slaughts of trouble. He was a levelheaded thinker
who did not emotionally blame God when things
went badly. He figured that much of the difficulty
was his own fault. "The rest was just the way things
bounced," he said. "You have to expect some setbacks."

He applied strict reason to his situation, carefully
thinking out better procedures, analyzing his mistakes, trying to eliminate the error factor. In fact,
he did everything that an intelligent man might
think of. But, even so, discouragement had, as he
explained, "grabbed him and just wouldn't let go."
Slowly but certainly he was yielding to depression.
It was infiltrating his thought and control center,
and his strong faith was beginning to erode.

But suddenly Harold "took corrective action." That

phrase is not his or mine. I heard it from my friend Jim Knapp, and I have quoted it often. When I heard Jim use it, the wisdom of it struck me. Really, the way out of any defeatist situation is to stand up to it with strength, common sense, and spiritual guidance and take corrective action. *Action* is the key word. Right action corrects rightly.

And *that* is an important fact. It is not what happens to you that matters. It is what you think about what has happened to you. When you begin to think right, objectively rather than emotionally, positively rather than negatively, you can resolutely take corrective action.

Since a thought is something that goes on in your mind and something that you can control if you have the will to do so, and discouragement is an accumulation of gloomy thoughts, you can choose to either entertain these thoughts or throw them out. That was the down-to-earth conclusion my friend reached. It made sense to him because when he directed discouraging thoughts to get out, they actually obeyed. Of course, they tried to fight back, but he faced them with power. In time he was on top of them. "Action was what I took. Just plain, old action. I was fed up with moaning and grumbling and the self-pity that goes with that type of nonthinking. Action, action, and more action, corrective action, that is the idea," he declared exultantly.

"What form did your action take? Just what was your corrective action?" I asked. It seems that it first took the form of physical action. He stopped slumping and sitting around dismally going over and over in his mind, "Why me?" He went out and walked and walked; he swam and swam; he began hitting golf balls again. This action took the strain off the cerebral center that governs thought and shifted it to physical activity. His mind began to clear, he felt better, the blood surged through his veins, and his heart rate accelerated. As he walked and stepped up physical activity, he was taking action, and he began to think eagerly not glumly. Ideas began popping up in his mind. Then one day the moment came when he exclaimed jubilantly, "Why I can work out of this!" He recovered his normal verve, not immediately to be sure, but it did not take as long as one might assume. When a person takes strong corrective, vigorous action, things soon begin to improve.

Following the physical action came an upgraded mental attitude and thought process. Harold looked in succession at each trouble or setback and asked what each one had to tell him. He fell back on a phrase I had quoted in one of my books, that great statement by W. Clement Stone, "To every disadvantage there is a corresponding advantage." So my friend scrupulously and diligently looked for advantages in what seemed hopeless disadvantages. He was surprised to find quite a few that subsequently turned into successes. With his new positive spirit everything looked better, and things began to go better for him. Action had driven off the dull inertness created by his negative mental attitude of discouragement.

An old friend of Harold's said, "Haven't seen you lately. Where have you been hibernating?"

"I've been licking my wounds," Harold replied, "but, thank God, I'm coming out of a rough down period."

To which his friend said, "You're thanking the right person. I've found that you can pray and praise your way out of any setback and discouraging condition." Harold said he followed the praying bit, but he wasn't sure he understood the praise part. The friend stated his belief that rough going is one of God's ways of teaching us something, of helping us to grow big. He had found that praising the Lord opens up new meanings of adversity. Harold took up this new idea and added the prayer and praise action to his physical and positive mental action. He discovered that in doing so, a balanced corrective action plan lifted the dark curtain of discouragement even further. Ultimately he became his normal self again. The alternative to the corrective action treatment Harold employed might have been failure and breakdown. But it didn't happen that way. This man did not break when adversity came; he responded by breaking new records.

His story reminds me of another friend of long-standing. I refer to the late great merchant J. C. Penney. He achieved notable success out of poverty but was dogged by adversity over much of his successful career. I knew him quite well. One day it occurred to me to ask him, "J. C., please give in one sentence the secret of your success in life."

"I can do that in four words—adversity and Jesus Christ." He explained that adversity made a man of him and that Jesus Christ was his Savior and guide.

My total memory of J. C. Penney, who lived to well up his nineties, is that of a happy man. He drew his happiness from his strong Christian faith. Only once did I know him to become discouraged or depressed. It was following one of the greatest adversities in his business life. He was in the depths of despair, utterly disconsolate.

Then off in the distance he heard singing. It was an old favorite hymn, "Be not dismayed whate'er betide, God will take care of you." Suddenly his discouragement lifted, and as by a miracle, he was set free from its devastating effect.

Years later when I spoke at his funeral service, that same hymn was sung at his request. He believed that God would take care of him, that Jesus Christ was at his side. In that faith he conquered discouragement. J. C. Penney was a convinced, practicing positive thinker made so through hardship and the belief that God will help anyone who thinks and has faith.

Positive thinking is vital to the processes that are guaranteed to keep your spirit always high, so high indeed that discouragement cannot break it. The positive thinker is a creative thinker, a cool, objective thinker in whatever situation he finds himself. He is never emotionally overwhelmed by problems. He knows that every problem contains the seeds of its own solution, that in all difficulty there is buried some great possibility. Therefore, to him a problem is not inherently bad, something to flee or avoid. It is a challenge or an opportunity containing some inherent good. When an apparently tough problem presents itself, he is not frightened by it, certainly not discouraged by any lack of ability to handle it. Instead, he stands up to it, believes it may contain amazingly great values, and humbly knows that he has what it takes to extract those values from it. Problems are men makers, women makers, life makers.

If the problem or difficulty may temporarily prove baffling, defying his best efforts to effect a solution, the true positive thinker does not get discouraged and walk away from it in defeat. It is not in his nature to give way to discouragement or to take a licking. He just sticks with it, believing that there is an answer for every problem. This characteristic is sometimes called persistence or perseverance or stick-to-itiveness. Call it what you will, in addition to faith, it is the chief enemy of discouragement and always wins over it, if maintained.

I have indicated earlier that in my working life, it has been my good fortune never to have an easy job. I have been the pastor of four churches, and when I started with each of them, they were heavily in debt and low in membership and had an unpromising, even doubtful, future. Each was at the bottom, but the bottom is a propitious place to be because the only direction from there is up. I cannot overemphasize that fact. If you take a job that is already up, you must keep it up or lift it higher. To me, that hardly affords the satisfaction found in taking on a job that is down, perhaps way down, and bringing it up, way up. That is good fortune indeed.

Now I must admit that in the case of each of these four jobs I got plenty discouraged, but in each church I met persons from whom I learned much. Out of the situation I formed the technique of positive thinking. Trouble, difficulty, and hardship are three great teachers. Fortunate is the person who in keeping company with them keeps his eyes, his ears and, better still, his mind open; they can teach him valuable things.

Four significant ideas were given to me along the way, ideas that helped me to gain a lasting victory over discouragement.

1. Never build a case against yourself.
2. Love the Lord and love people. Forget yourself.
3. Think big, pray big, believe big, act big, love big, be big—big all the way.
4. Be a believer—a believer in God. Be a believer in people, in the future. Be a believer in yourself.

Positive thinkers become discouraged at times simply because they are human beings. As I pointed out earlier, all men and women are affected by the rise and fall of moods, by the variableness of emotional reactions. But positive thinkers develop the mental and spiritual capacity to keep their thinking operative, whatever the situation. They are mentally controlled rather than emotionally conditioned. As a result, even though positive thinkers may at times experience discouragement, by their sound, mentally controlled, and objective attitude, they are able to rise above the discouragement and handle it. Nor do positive thinkers accept an attitude of discouragement as the final answer to a failure situation of any kind. They forget it and try again.

On a plane en route to a speaking engagement at a business convention, I sat by a pleasant fellow who said that he was the principal speaker at the same meeting where I was scheduled to speak. "I thought that I was the principal speaker," I replied, laughingly. He then announced that he was a humorist, a comic, and produced one of his folders that billed him as the "funniest speaker in the world, the funniest man alive." One of the captions was "Hang onto your seats, folks, for he will rock you into the aisles." Another was "Hold your sides. You're going to die laughing."

"Believe me," I said, "I hope I come on first. I certainly don't want to follow you." But as it turned out, the humorist was the first speaker, and I was to follow him.

The emcee of the evening went all out in describing my fellow speaker. He used extravagant phrases, assuring the audience that they were in for the time of their lives. But apparently he built the speaker up too highly. The humorist got good laughs, but they began to taper off to titters, finally to grins. Perspiring but undaunted, he said to me out of the corner of his mouth, "Tough crowd." Finally he gave it up and sat down to rather perfunctory applause. "Whew," he said as he mopped his face, "hard going for sure."

I had no better luck when my turn came to speak. Again the effusive emcee went all out in the introduction. To hear him talk, you would have thought I was the greatest speaker who ever orated. Such is human nature that the more he eulogized me, the more the audience wanted to know "who is this guy?" Sensing the cooling-off mood of the crowd, I decided to try no jokes at all, though I do have a few that always seem to get a good response. I used nothing but serious material. The trouble was that the audience laughed when they were not supposed to. "Tough crowd," I said to my friend out of the side of my mouth. They gave me a fair hand, but I knew it was out of generosity.

On the way back to the hotel, the humorist said, "I'm discouraged, are you?"

"Well, I'm not exactly elated."

"Tell you what," he continued. "Let's forget it, wipe it out, relegate it to the past. Have you a speaking engagement tomorrow night?" When I said that I did, he nodded. "That's good. So have I. Let's take the positive attitude that we will do better next time." Then he added a wise remark that has stayed with me: go after a success after every failure. That is the way a positive thinker handles a failure situation. It is also the way a positive thinker wins over discouragement. This leads us directly into Chapter 8 in which one important characteristic of a positive thinker is discussed: how the positive thinker drops the negative word habit.

8.

Drop the Negative Word Habit

POSITIVE THINKERS are word droppers. They drop every negative word that gets in the way of personal growth and development—words such as *if, can't,* and *impossible.* They simply and forthrightly chuck them out of their vocabulary and thinking.

A negative word is a symbol of a negative concept that can be harmful. Dropping it is of superimportance. In fact, it is good to go so far as to bury such failure-generating words.

One man I heard of did just that. A group of people purchased land on which to build a big human service institution. But, as always, some among them doubted that it could be done. They said, "If we had more support, if we had more money, if . . . if . . . if." More enterprises and more people have probably gone down to failure on the little word *if* than any other, unless it is the word *can't.*

Others in the group discouragingly opined, "It

can't be done. There is just no way. It can't be done, can't ... can't ... can't."

Still others were even more explicit. "It's impossible," they declared. "No way can we accomplish it. It is impossible ... impossible ... impossible." So the deadening, negative words droned on hopelessly.

But one positive, innovative man came up with a unique idea. He was a generous donor to the undertaking, and when he asked for a little piece of land that had been acquired, his request could not very well be denied. But everyone was curious and surprised when he explained that he wanted it for a "cemetery." He fenced off the little enclosure and set three small gravestones.

At the announced time for the burial service, people were assembled, and he unveiled the stones. In one was carved the word *If,* in another *Can't,* and in the third *Impossible.* "Here lie buried words that could cause the failure of our enterprise. Leave them buried," he said. The people got the message.

This creative outcome was due to a positive thinker, a word dropper. He dropped and buried those negative and defeating words.

The famous psychiatrist, Dr. Smiley Blanton, noted how often patients would think back glumly "if only I had not done that," "if only I had done that," one futile "if only" after another. His imaginative treatment was successful. He instructed each patient to imagine an opening in the head from which a recording of the words *if only* could be removed and the words *next time* inserted. The patient was to "listen" intently until he heard the click of the new recording in place. This imaging process proved remarkably successful in eliminating the negative "if only" concept and in substituting the positive "next time" affirmation.

The thoughts, ideas, and concepts that lodge in our minds result in attitudes and beliefs, and these in turn determine whether we experience failure or success. The "if only" attitude is a despairing, totally ineffective look back at something that has gone by: if only I had bought that stock; if only I had not sold when I did; if only I had taken that job; if only I had not nagged my husband so much that he left me; if only I had not mistreated my wife. I'm sure you could come up with some examples too.

The positive thinker is free from all such futile recriminations. His idea is not "if only." It is a much stronger, forward-looking idea, one full of hope and expectation. It is the dynamic thought, "next time." With this concept he gets unlimited positive results. If he makes a mistake, doesn't do what he should have done, or does what he should not have done he turns his back on all of it and simply affirms, "Next time I will do better, act more wisely. Next time I will have improved judgment." "Next time" thinking is geared to going forward, to doing better! Do not be an "if only" thinker because that is related to the past—to mistakes, errors, losses, bad judgments, situations that you can no longer do anything about.

My wife, Ruth, once met a Dakota farmer at a church dinner on the western plains late one summer. As national president of her denominational board of domestic missions, she was a speaker at a church conference. Seated across the table from the farmer at dinner, she tried to engage him in conversation, but he was not very articulate, obviously unaccustomed to small talk. Seeking to identify with his interests, she asked, "How are the crops this year?"

"Not good, ma'am. In fact, there aren't any crops. I saved maybe 10 percent of my crop, but my brother lost everything."

Appalled, my wife asked, "But what happened?"

"We had a tornado. In ten minutes everything was gone." Then he was silent.

"But what do you do when everything goes bad like that, sir?"

"Do?" he paused as if looking deeply into his mind. "Do? Why we just aim to forget it."

This man had lived with nature for years. He had lived with the element of wind, cold, heat, and tornadoes. He had experienced good years and bad. He worked in partnership with God, the Creator, who gave us the good earth and who watches over us in the good and the bad times. This man of stature had calmly accepted the fortuitous and the devastating as facts of life. He did not pathetically cry "if only," but sturdily determined that next time he would go forward. He always regrouped, he always went forward, building, ever building.

He fitted the definition of a positive thinker: one who is tough and rugged mentally and spiritually, who sees every difficulty but sees it straight. He knows that ultimately the good in this world overbalances the evil. He knows that with the help of the good God, he has what it takes to take it. He finds the answer and always overcomes.

When the ifs and the can'ts and the impossibles gang up on you, what then? Why, just counter with the next times and the cans and the possibles. It is that simple, though it isn't all that easy. Sometimes it can be hard, very hard indeed, but if you persevere, think positively, and have faith, you will come through a winner, perhaps even a big winner.

Furthermore, you learn to be a philosopher. Often what seem to be destructive adversities turn out to be creative assets, and those assets would not have become yours if something hadn't happened that at first seemed to ruin everything for you. When things go wrong, ultimately they may turn out right. So when your hopes and dreams and goals get dashed, poke around among the wreckage. You may find your golden opportunity in what seems to be ruin.

Remember the story of Mordecai Brown, one of the greatest big league baseball pitchers of his time? His parents were very poor, but like real Americans, they never really knew they were. Their son had his heart set on being a big league pitcher, and he showed extraordinary talent at a young age. Mordecai worked on a farm to help support his family as did other kids in those days. One day he got his hand caught in some machinery and lost most of the forefinger on his right hand and badly crushed his second finger.

"There goes all my hope of being a pitcher," so the negative thinker would moan. "If only I hadn't had that accident. Now I can't pitch with that ruined hand. Out the window go my dreams. It's just impossible." But that was not the way this boy thought and talked. He accepted it and got along with that poor hand as best he could. He learned to throw the ball with the fingers he had left. Eventually he made a local team as third baseman.

One day the team manager happened to be directly behind the first baseman when Mordecai threw from third. He was astounded to watch the twists and turns, the amazing gyrations of that ball as it sped true into the first baseman's mitt. "Mordecai," he said enthusiastically, "you are a born pitcher. You have speed and control and, boy, with that gyrating ball you'll have every batter swinging but only hitting the air."

Mordecai would throw the ball in such a way that it would come fast, dancing, twisting, turning, gyrating up and down, sliding directly over the plate. The batters were totally baffled. Mordecai mowed down the batting order. His strikeout record was impressive as were his games won. He became one of the great pitchers of American baseball.

How did this boy accomplish this feat of turning disaster into an asset? Those injured fingers, the abbreviated forefinger and gnarled second finger, gave the ball those extraordinary twists and turns. This boy, a believer raised in a faith-filled home, simply believed that he could take what he had and make something of it. He was a positive thinker who, with incredible skill, handled his life's impossibles. His word dropping—tossing out the ifs, the can'ts, and the impossibles—made him a baseball immortal.

Now I know you might say, "I'm no superperson like Mordecai Brown. I can't come back from hard luck like he did." But when Mordecai had the accident to his hand, he was no superperson either. The plain fact is that all of us have far more qualifications than we realize. Just affirm those creative words—*next time, can,* and *possible.* And be like every good positive thinker, be a word dropper and throw out *if, can't,* and *impossible.*

In addition, fasten your mind onto another word, a victory word, an overcoming, wonder-working word—*miracle.* The positive thinker is a believer. He believes that nothing is too good to be true, so he believes in miracles.

A negative-thinking man was married to a positive-thinking woman. This was back in the depression time, and like most families, they had problems, mostly financial. He griped steadily, "If we could only work out of this situation, I could see our way through this. It's all impossible."

But the positive-thinking wife sang a different tune, "How do we go about solving this problem? I know we can handle this one. It is no real problem. It's perfectly possible." The two loved each other, and she pulled him along, supplying faith and optimism for both. He managed to hold onto his job while a lot of others were losing theirs. Her faith in him had a lot to do with this.

He worked in a shop where merchandise from Great Britain was sold, mostly woolens. This man, Henry, was undoing a package of goods one day, and on top of the contents he found a folded piece of paper. He picked it up and read, "Expect a miracle—it can happen." *Wonder who wrote that and why?* he said to himself. He started to toss it in the wastebasket, but something stopped him. *Guess I'll show it to Helen. She falls for fool stuff like this.* He put the paper in his pocket.

That night he shoved it across the table. "Honey, funny thing. Some oddball in Britain put this message in a box I was opening today. Kind of a nut, I guess."

She read it, then sat thoughtfully looking down at it. "No, Henry, I don't think the person who put this in that box was an oddball and certainly not a nut. He or she must have had some sort of trouble, maybe like the ones we have, and was guided to pass it along in this curious manner to help someone else, us, for example.

"We haven't been able to see our way through some things. Tell you what. Let's take one of our small problems and really expect a miracle, test it out, so to speak."

"Oh, come off it, honey. A miracle is some dreamy-eyed, goofy thing that only happens in fairy tales. Miracles don't happen in this scientific age." And they were off on one of their friendly arguments.

Helen went to the bookcase. "Let's see what our friend Mr. Webster says about miracles." She read from the dictionary, "*Miracle*—'a wonderful happening.' And," she declared triumphantly, "it doesn't say anything about its being contrary to science. I wonder if we call something a miracle simply because we do not understand it. And when we do understand, then it is part of the whole scientific body of knowledge. Airplanes were once in the category of miracles. They were wonderful happenings. The electric lights were too, and the telephone. Someday what we now call miracles, like healing outside the known laws of medicine and psychic phenomena, will all be part of scientific law. And finally," she concluded, "perhaps we will come to realize that even faith itself is part of the laws of God, the Creator who made them all."

"Smart girl" was all Henry could manage to respond. "You could be right." So the two agreed they would expect a miracle, a wonderful happening in connection with one of their smaller problems. They brought positive thought to bear, her strong positive attitude, his weaker one. But even a weak positive thought pattern is not without power, as is taught in Matthew 17:20, "If you have faith as a mustard seed, . . . nothing will be impossible for you."

Sometime later Henry and Helen had occasion to be thankful for a rather strange series of coincidences and circumstances. The matter to which they applied the "expect a miracle—it can happen" principle began to work out. The outcome was not exactly what they wanted or thought they needed, but it proved to be a right answer. Even Henry came to believe in miracles. But Helen, a positive-thinking word dropper, was responsible for starting miracles working in their lives by dropping the idea of the impossible and concentrating on the possible. There came a time when Henry also became a full-fledged positive thinker. He came to it the hard way, but when he became convinced that we become what we think and that what we think comes to us, he joined his wife in positive thinking. They became a really effective team of positive thinkers who got positive results.

Positive thinking brings the best values to those who are dedicated to achieving the best. And we all, I believe, want the best for ourselves and for our families. Would you like to have the best, or are you actually willing to settle for something less than the best? Of course, you would choose the best. How can you have that best? Think the best, not the worst, because in the long run you tend to get what you think.

If you really want to know what you are likely to be five or ten years from now, all you need to do is read the thoughts that are now dominant in your mind. In time the continuity of your dominant thought pattern will activate the forces about you to produce the outward conditions that correspond to your basic thinking. Your thoughts form your future. Thoughts externalize into actualization. You cannot see a thought, but you can trace its effect. And all your thoughts add up to a result. In due course you become precisely what you habitually think.

The positive thinker succeeds in life. As a word dropper, he has cast out of his life-style a pernicious mental sickness called negative expectation, always expecting things to be bad.

Common expressions that indicate negative expectation are "things always go wrong for me," "I know I can't make it," "it's going to be a lousy day." Some people actually think they were born to lose. Negative-thinking parents render a profound disservice to their children by conditioning their minds to failure, though they do so unwittingly.

A young woman stopped me on the way out of an auditorium where I had just finished a talk on positive thinking. She was very concerned about what she called a "longtime mind-set" from which she was trying to extricate herself. "Ever since childhood I've had a failure pattern. I would do well in school when it began in the fall, but some weeks later I would start doing badly. From then on I would go down until I was failing in my work. Often I just plain flunked," she said hopelessly.

After finishing school a year behind her class, she got a job. She was a pretty girl and had a nice way about her that enabled her to make a good first impression but eventually the old failure pattern "would grab her" again.

I asked, "What do you think is the cause of this deeply rooted failure pattern that holds you back?"

She hesitated, "I hate to blame anyone and hope I'm not being unfair, but to tell the truth, I think it's my mother's fault. Oh, I don't want to say this because Mother is really wonderful and I love her. But ever since I was little, she was always talking about her worries. She was negative thinker number one. For her, nothing was ever going to turn out right. Everything was bound to turn out badly. She used to say, 'Honey, you might as well expect the worst so you won't be disappointed.' So I guess I have always been subconsciously expecting the worst and I haven't been disappointed. But I sure am an unhappy person. What can I do?"

As I listened to this unhappy and mixed-up but obviously bright young woman trying desperately to find herself, I admired her perceptiveness. She recognized that she was caught in a self-defeating complex of thought, one that was deeply rooted in her consciousness. I suggested that the mental roots of negative expectation had to be cut. Then they would wither, and she could pull them out of her mind like persistent weeds in the lawn.

My impression of her sharpness was verified by the alacrity with which she picked up the figure of speech I had used, "roots of negative expectation." "But give me a prescription right now for getting release," she declared. "I just know you can."

"With all your negativism, you're pretty positive about this," I said with a smile. "So let's try."

"Any ingrained, long-held habit can be eliminated and a healthy thought pattern substituted if you will do the following: (1) Want such change to take place. An all-out intensity of desire is the first requirement. It must be more than a half-hearted wish. (2) Know specifically how you want to be different. In your case you want to substitute a success thought pattern for your hitherto dominant failure pattern. (3) Fix an exact time when you will start the process of eliminating the failure pattern and also when you expect the success pattern to be established."

"Oh," she exclaimed, "I already know about that. I will start now, and the date for the change is today, right now."

"Hold your horses," I replied, "we are not talking about an easy process. Mental habits are formed slowly and have been intricately wound around in your subconsciousness. The unwinding process takes time."

"But," she said, "I remember reading about you, Dr. Peale, having an awful inferiority complex. You prayed to the Lord and reminded Him that He could change thieves into honest people and drunks into sober people and that He could also do that right off."

"Yes," I agreed, "and I believe that, but the Lord didn't do that right off in my case. He took a while with me. I was a tough case, but He did change me and He will change you too."

Then I continued: "(4) Start right now visualizing or imaging yourself as you want to be. See yourself as having dropped that old failure pattern and as now taking on a vital, dynamic success pattern. (5)

Begin at once practicing the 'as if' principle. If you want to be something that you are not, act as if you possess the desired quality. If this is done with persistence, you will ultimately attain this quality. In your case, begin now to act as if you are success oriented. Acting as if it is so can make it so. (6) You are now ready for the dynamic process of life changing through faith. Acknowledge to the Lord that you cannot effect such profound personal change on your own. The Bible says, 'If you can believe, all things are possible' (Mark 9:23). If you can believe, and if you want to and will to, ask the Lord who created you to re-create you. If you have faith that such a result will happen, it will happen."

This is not fanciful, dreamy-eyed, nor some sort of religious stuff. This process has worked over centuries for millions of people and works today in this modern world. Had it been only a theory or a vague unsubstantiated claim, it would have been discredited long ago. But the validity of spiritual and mental change of personality is recognized widely as scientific (it works) reality. The young woman whose experience is related here is just one example of a person who, by a process of idea dropping and substitution, became a new person. She put this process into operation. She did not find change to be quick or easy, but it did come gradually and the goal she set was eventually attained. She did eliminate the long-held failure pattern. She became successful in her occupation, but more important, she became successful as a person.

If we take on wrong ideas, we can also drop wrong

ideas. If we grow into wrong thought patterns, we can, if we want to and will to, drop the erroneous thought patterns. And if we are motivated by real desire, we can take on a new, more positive life-style. There is extraordinary power in creative positive expectation.

Life can be a wonderful, satisfying experience. Despite all of its adversities, life itself is good. Believe in the value of life and its infinite worth. Built in it, for those who believe and endure, are ultimate joy, peace, and achievement. Fulfillment is offered to all by almighty God, the Creator and the Re-Creator of all who want the good for their lives.

Unfortunately some people fail to see the great values of life because of sadly twisted thought processes. A chief reason I write about having faith and practicing positive thinking and finally winning over every form of defeat and adversity is that I believe in life and love it. I want to encourage others to believe in it and love it too.

USA Today carried a full-page story about teenage suicides. The writer said, "Nearly everybody seems to have a theory about the cause: drugs, alcohol, sex, unemployment, child abuse, divorce, the decline of churchgoing, pressure to achieve, conflict with parents, the threat of nuclear war, excessive television watching, the availability of handguns, biochemical imbalances. But nobody has a satisfactory answer."

But one writer in the same issue, Don Wildmon, has come up with sound reasoning, I believe. He asks:

Why are we suffering from this tragedy? Because for the past two decades our society has been on a hedonistic binge, placing materialism and self-indulgence high on our scale of values. We have tended to play down man's spiritual nature. . . . Mass media, especially television, no longer allow the child to be a child, or the adolescent to be adolescent. By exposing them continually to an adult world, which is basically materialistic, we have robbed children of the privilege of childhood. They have been told over and over again that things bring happiness and that happiness is the chief goal in life. We have sold our youth a big lie. . . . What can we do? Restore time-proven, traditional Christian values. . . . Expose hedonism for what it is—a big lie, a mirage that always fades.*

Hedonism—the concept that the primary aim of life is sensory pleasure—is, of course, a crude falsehood, a bold lie. The truth about life is found not in the cynical mutterings of the unwashed but in the clean facts of the Bible: "Whoever finds me [the Lord] finds life" (Prov. 8:35) and "I [Jesus] have come that they may have life, and that they may have it more abundantly" (John 10:10). So positive thinkers who are smart enough to spot a lie are again ruthless, sophisticated word droppers. They drop hedonism into the garbage can where it belongs and go on being happy, actually reveling in

*Copyright, 1983 USA TODAY. Reprinted with permission.

life. Positive thinkers love life and do something wonderful with it every day.

As I write this chapter, I am at a convention to give two talks. The meeting is composed of hundreds of people, each of whom achieved over a million dollars of sales last year and won a trip to this convention.

Mingling with these people who became outstanding achievers, I heard story after story of men and women who dropped negative thoughts, negative attitudes, negative ideas. They cast them out and turned their backs on defeatist concepts. They embraced the positive. They went to work. They believed. They visualized. They worked and worked, believed and believed. They became winners and achievers, and they and their families found great happiness in the process. And that is exactly what you can do.

One man who attended this convention unhesitatingly told me, "I don't deserve any credit for my performance. My wife made me a successful man. She pulled me out of a failure psychology and got me going."

The wife standing by said, "Don't you believe it. He has always been a great man. All I did was to remind him of what and who he is."

It seems that this man was a self-doubter. He felt inadequate. He didn't believe that he could. He had a low and erroneous opinion of his abilities and potential. Gradually his daily conversation was filled with downbeat ideas and negative expressions: "It won't work," "Yeah, maybe he can do it, but I can't," "Guess I'm no good at this job." When awards for top performance were given, he would come up with a classic negativism, "I can't see myself ever winning an award." Classic because it indicated he had never imaged or visualized himself succeeding.

Well, at breakfast one morning when he was glumly getting off his usual negatives, his wife really reacted. "Listen," she said, "I'm going to tell you something. You make me tired with all that put-down stuff. I know you, and you are a very able, indeed a superior and effective person, and you are constantly lying to yourself about yourself. I am sick of it. I'm fed up with your negative conversation. If it were true, I'd go along with it, but since it's all untrue, I'm insisting that you stop it."

Her husband started to interrupt this flow of wifely indignation, but she said, "I'm not through with you yet. I love you, I know you in and out, and I believe in you. I am not going to stand by and watch you destroy yourself by a stupid inferiority complex. For heaven's sake, start thinking positively. Be a man and stand up to yourself." She concluded blazingly, "I won't listen to this negative talk any more."

She really got to her husband. Basically he knew she was right. Now, afraid to speak any more negatives, he found he had to talk positively. In time he began to try thinking positively. Then he tried positive action. He tried and tried and finally succeeded. His sales topped a million dollars that year. He became a prize winner. That is how I happened to meet him at the convention. He put his arm around his wife's shoulders and looked down at her proudly, "Isn't it great to have a wife who makes you be what she knows you can be?"

In the next chapter I will show you how positive thinking relates to vital aspects of your life, health, and energy.

9.

Positive Secrets of Health and Energy

GOD WANTS you to have the best of life all your life. He wants you to feel a glorious aliveness—physically, mentally, and spiritually. Jesus said, "I have come that they may have life, and that they may have it more abundantly" (John 10:10). Or, as another translation, the Good News Bible, puts it, "I have come in order that you might have life—life in all its fullness" (TEV).

Do you have a vibrant quality in your life? Or are you only fractionally alive, only partially healthy? Does your energy run out, leaving you tired, even exhausted?

If this describes you, this chapter is for you. It offers no advice about diet or physical exercise. Nor is it medical advice, since I am not a doctor of medicine. It outlines ways that can produce vibrant health and abundant energy every day. It is not theoretical because I have personally tested every suggestion offered. I make no claim to have been a great athlete or superstrong man, but I have had good, sound health and great reserves of energy all my life, energy that has never run down. I think my good health and great energy are the result of my sincerely attempting to base my life on spiritual laws and principles found in the Bible—principles that never change. They have always helped me, and now I hope they will help you.

I have always taught faith as an important way to a good, healthy life. Now leading medical men are speaking of the health-producing "faith factor." Herbert Benson, M.D., says:

I'm not at all interested in promoting one religious or philosophical system over another . . . I'm most concerned with the scientifically observable phenomena and forces that accompany faith. . . . My research and that of others has disclosed that those who develop and use the Faith Factor effectively can:

- Relieve headaches
- Reduce angina pectoris pains and perhaps even eliminate the need for bypass surgery (an estimated 80 percent of angina pain can be relieved by positive belief!)
- Enhance creativity, especially when experiencing some sort of "mental block"
- Overcome insomnia
- Prevent hyperventilation attacks
- Reduce blood pressure and help control hypertension problems
- Enhance the therapy of cancer
- Control panic attacks

- Lower cholesterol levels
- Alleviate the symptoms of anxiety that include nausea, vomiting, diarrhea, constipation, short temper, and inability to get along with others
- Reduce overall stress and achieve great inner peace and emotional balance

The Faith Factor should be used in conjunction with modern medicine. It should be an addition to the awesome cures that the medical profession can now perform. The two approaches—the Faith Factor *and* modern medicine—can enhance each other's impact and, together, bring about optimal results (*Beyond the Relaxation Response* [New York: Times Books, 1975], p. 88).

We live in a material world, and, of course, the material world is important. We couldn't survive without it. But we also live in a mental and spiritual world, and that is even more important. A psychiatrist once said, "Attitudes are more important than facts." That is another way of saying that the world of ideas is just as real and significant as the world of material things.

It is also true that an underlying force, or power, links the material, mental, and spiritual worlds. Your awareness and acknowledgment of this force have much to do with your degree of health and the amount of energy you have in life.

Let me tell you about a woman whose life was turned around. She was only thirty-four years old, supposedly in the prime of life. But, because of frail health, she could do no housework, and she was considered too delicate to have a child. She often took to her bed for lengthy intervals, her energy at low level.

The negative and apprehensive thought pattern thus created siphoned off her joy in living and contributed to her decline in health and energy. She developed into a perennial patient and was a familiar figure in doctors' offices. Her husband sadly accepted the conclusion that he had a semi-invalid wife whose life expectancy was limited.

She was a nominal Christian and a regular church-goer. Her religious training and upbringing had given her a sincere faith in prayer. She accepted the teaching that guidance in solving problems could come through prayer. Gradually, as she prayed for help in her physical problem, she began to believe that an answer would come.

One day, while reading the Bible, she had a thought that amazed her. It is one now commonly accepted, but then it was revolutionary in concept. And her thought was this: physical health can actually be strengthened or weakened, even gained or lost, depending upon one's basic, continuous mental attitude.

In a flash, the insight came to her that as one thinks or images in deep consciousness, so will one tend to become. This independently conceived idea burst with life-changing force into her mind. It was a revelation. Without any involved or complex process of reasoning, she perceived the truth of this idea with such clarity that she accepted it totally.

On a spring day immediately following this mental and spiritual experience, she was walking along a quiet tree-lined street with her husband. The trees were in bud, and the reemerging life of nature was dramatically in evidence everywhere. Suddenly she stopped, "I see it. I see it. That's it!" she exclaimed. "It is the life-force, the wonderful life-force!"

Her startled husband asked, "What do you mean, the life-force?"

She pointed to the leaves bursting from buds, to the brown grass turning green, to the jonquils, hyacinths, and daffodils pushing up from the soil. "That," she declared, "is the life-force. And that same marvelous, re-creative power of new life is in people too. It has to be. Aren't human beings the highest form of creation? They can be re-created by the same miracle of new life." As she spoke, she seemed to be transformed. Her heightened color and dancing eyes attested to a new aliveness within her.

Suddenly she declared aloud, "I affirm that the life-force of almighty God, my Creator, is now re-creating me. This powerful life-force is surging into my mind, my heart, my bloodstream, all through my being. Health, energy, vitality, and new life are now being renewed in me just as in the trees, the grass, the flowers."

By an act of intense thought, belief, affirmation, and developing faith, this woman began the process of rejecting semi-invalidism and frailty. She acquired, in time, rugged health and energy that enabled her to live an outstanding, very busy life for ninety-six years. She became strong and healthy of body, clear and sharp of mind, enthusiastic and dynamic of spirit. And her faith-filled life inspired thousands until her triumphant departure to the higher life just four years short of a century.

It is amazing how sturdy health may be developed through a combination of insight, belief, in-depth faith, and affirmation of the re-creative power of the Creator. To reach and tap this endless source of energy, repeat or affirm aloud the following words at least once every day. As you do so, stand tall, take a deep breath, and say:

I am vigorous.
I am vitally alive.
I am filled with boundless energy.
I am radiant with good health.
I am joyful.
I am enthusiastic.
I am filled with the life-force.
I know that in Him is life and His life-force is at work in me,
    giving me health and energy and power.
Praise His holy name!

As you do this faithfully, believing sincerely, you will be taking creative spiritual action, and the power of the spiritual universe will flow toward you.

God wants you to be well, to be vital and vigorous all of your life. Believe that. Give thanks for it every day, saying aloud: "God wants me to be well." The Bible confirms this: "Beloved, I pray that you may prosper in all things and be in health, just as your soul prospers" (3 John 2).

In creating the human body, God made the most intricate, amazing instrument ever devised, packing into it complex organs designed to last for long years and work perfectly in a harmonious, balanced whole. To that He added a brain, consisting of about three pounds of tissue, able to think, reason, remember, conceive ideas, and produce noble works. To top it all off, God placed at the center of each human being a spirit or soul by which he or she can know the Creator and live with Him through time and eternity. Amazing!

The verse from 3 John relates the health of the body to the health of the soul. If the soul and the mind are kept free of evil, negative thoughts and attitudes, the body will be healthy. On the other hand, sickness of the soul can result in death: "The soul who sins shall die" (Ezek. 18:4).

Today we know that sickness of soul can result in bodily illness, but people were not really aware of this fact a generation or so ago. I remember well the first time the connection was made plain to me. As the young pastor of a church in Brooklyn, New York, I was called to a hospital to see a patient who was very ill. This man was a well-known politician, prominent in the community. His doctor told me that he was a devoted family man and a pillar of the church. The doctor also admitted that he was puzzled by the man's failure to respond to treatment. "Something seems to be blocking my attempts to cure him," the doctor said.

When I saw the man and looked into his lackluster eyes, I had the feeling that something was wrong with him spiritually, that the illness was spiritually based. I was very young and somewhat hesitant, but I said to him, "I know you are a man of good reputation, but tell me: is there something on your mind that is troubling you?"

He looked at me for what seemed a long time. Finally, in a tremulous voice, he said, "Yes, there is. I know I'm considered a good family man. I'm a deacon in my church, and I have a position of trust in government. And yet I have done things of which I am ashamed. To put it bluntly, I'm a sinner and a hypocrite. If people really knew me, nobody would respect me."

I offered him a threefold solution to his problem: penitence, confession, and restitution, after which would come forgiveness, peace, and healing. I listened to a recital of the sins he had committed, the wrongs he had done. Then he humbly asked for forgiveness. When he finished and I told him that God loved him and had forgiven him, he gave a deep sigh. "I feel so much better," he murmured. "I think I can sleep now."

That was the turning point in his illness. He recovered and went on to a useful, honorable life. The balance between body, mind, and soul was restored. He was made whole again.

This wholeness is what all of us should strive for at all times. Jesus taught us to ask God to deliver us from evil. When we sincerely ask for forgiveness, we are reborn and renewed—actually re-created in mind and soul. This process is described in Psalm 103:2–5:

> Bless the LORD, O my soul,
> And forget not all His benefits:
> Who forgives all your iniquities,
> Who heals all your diseases,
> Who redeems your life from destruction,
> Who crowns you with lovingkindness and
>   tender mercies,
> Who satisfies your mouth with good things,
> So that your youth is renewed like the eagle's.

Attaining health and energy is basically a spiritual process. The spiritual life stimulates vitality not only in the mind and the soul but also in the body. We become healthy to the degree to which the mind thinks healthy thoughts and the soul is morally clean. A clean soul actually sends continuing newness of health throughout the entire system.

In a clinical study of some 500 cases, it was found that 383 of the persons studied were sick, not because they had suffered accidents or organic diseases, but because, according to a doctor's vivid description, "Those patients were draining back into their bodies the diseased thoughts of their minds."

Generations ago Plato wrote: "Neither should we ever attempt to cure the body without curing the soul." Modern thinkers are just now realizing the sound thinking of this wise philosopher of ancient times.

Strive always for wholeness. Keep the three basic

elements of your being—body, mind, and soul—in harmony and balance. Remember that good health is possible only when these three elements work with, not against, each other.

Health, wholeness, holiness—these three words have a common origin. At the deepest level, they have a common meaning. Say this simple prayer:

> Lord, give me health.
> Lord, give me wholeness.
> Lord, give me holiness.

Those words will bring a deep peace and restfulness to your mind and body.

There is a powerful phrase in the book of Joshua: "Choose for yourselves this day whom you will serve" (24:15). The choice in those far-off times was between worshiping false gods or remaining faithful to the true God. But the challenge may also refer to many aspects of modern life. We make continual choices between the negative and the positive. We can choose a way of life that will bring us health and happiness, or we can choose the opposite. We can choose between faith and indifference. The choices really are endless.

Happiness, prosperity, and success in life really depend on making right choices, winning choices. There are forces in life working for you and others working against you. To have health and energy, you must be able to recognize beneficial and malevolent forces and choose correctly between them.

Every day when you arise, choices are waiting for

you. On the one hand are positive attitudes: creativity, enthusiasm, love, faith, hope. On the other hand are negative attitudes: hate, fear, worry, anger, anxiety. These negative attitudes will seize you if you permit them to do so. Once they fasten onto you, they will work steadily to produce negative results: loss of energy, loss of creativity, loss of enthusiasm and, ultimately, loss of health.

Fortunately, as an intelligent person, as a student of human nature, you can use the positive forces to maintain a healthy body and repel all negative forces. That is a crucial choice, a winning choice. Making this choice requires clear thinking and a strong, resolute faith. When faith declines, doubt takes over, and it can ultimately poison any personality. Dr. Charles Mayo said, "I never knew a man to die of overwork, but I have known many men to die of doubt."

I knew a woman whose eighty-seven-year-old father was killed in an accident crossing a highway. An autopsy revealed that this man had within him conditions that should have developed into serious illnesses. But they hadn't. The doctors told this woman, "Your father had all sorts of potential illnesses that might have progressed. Actually, he should have died twenty years ago. But you say that he was active and energetic as he approached ninety years of age. That's remarkable."

The woman said, "My father was in the habit of saying every morning, 'This is going to be a fine day!' If someone pointed out some ominous or threatening situation, his reply always was: 'I have hopes.' "

Obviously this man had the life-force working in him. In spite of the seeds of illness in him, his body was totally alive. His faith, vitality, enthusiasm, and love of life were more powerful than the negative forces of illness working against him.

The late Wilbur Cross, governor of Connecticut, had a similar outlook on life. Each day he would exclaim enthusiastically, "It's a great day for it!" Every day always had something great to offer—and when you stop to think about it, that is true. Each day is a great day for *something*.

Tomorrow, go to an open window, take a deep breath, look out at your particular corner of the world, and say aloud:

Thank You, God, for being alive.
Thank You for family and friends.
Today is going to be a great day.
I have high hopes for all that this day will bring.
I intend to live every minute of it fully.
The Lord made this day; I will rejoice and be glad in it!

Use this affirmation as a morning action-motivator. It will help make each day a great day.

Sometimes I am complimented on my energy. Actually that energy isn't mine at all. It comes because I try always to keep my mind open and receptive to the energy that comes to me from God the Re-Creator.

Once, after I had made an energetic speech of

some forty-five minutes, a reporter asked, "Where do you get all that vitality? What is the secret of your amazing energy?"

He probably expected some remarks about exercise, diet, sleep habits, or inherited characteristics. But I looked at him in silence for some moments. Finally I said, "Do you want to know the real secret of health and energy?"

"I sure do," he replied fervently.

"It is in the book of Isaiah, chapter forty, verse thirty-one":

> But those who wait on the LORD
> Shall renew their strength;
> They shall mount up with wings like eagles,
> They shall run and not be weary,
> They shall walk and not faint.

That one statement has had so much to do with my personal continuing health and energy that I suggest the use of it to anyone who really wants to be healthy and energetic. Strength is promised to "those who wait on the Lord." That means, of course, an attitude of belief that you will truly be healthy and strengthened by God Himself, as you center your life and concentrate your thoughts on Him.

The passage from Isaiah describes strength as a powerful upthrust akin to the takeoff of an eagle. Have you ever seen an eagle "mount up"? I did once, years ago in the Rocky Mountains. The gigantic bird was perched on a huge needle of stone, high up on a mountain, clutching the apex with rugged claws. It remained poised on that lofty perch for long minutes. Finally, spreading its wings to the fullest extent and sending out a reverberating scream, the eagle took off, heading up and up into the blue until, as a diminishing speck, it disappeared over a mountain peak. I found myself deeply moved, repeating the lines, "They shall mount up with wings like eagles."

But the Scripture passage reaches its climax not in the mounting up but in the steady continuance; "They shall run and not be weary, / They shall walk and not faint." The outcome of the mounting up is being able to walk in the tough, hard ways and keep going, always keep going.

As you rise up in thought and spirit like an eagle, you are given insight, stamina, and patience to maintain strength, energy, and determination to persevere no matter what difficulties may come upon you. And those energies derived from spiritual upthrust will not ever run down.

This truth is simple and basic, like all great truths. Those who wait on the Lord are putting themselves into the life-force that God has built into the universe. It is possible to exist on the edges of this great power, or even outside it; but that is mere existence, not real living. Every truly successful, happy person I have ever known recognizes this and opts for the life-force.

For those who are unsure of what is meant by that phrase, "wait on the Lord," the Lord Himself has provided rules and guidelines spelled out so clearly that anyone can understand them. That is why reading the Bible regularly is important. It offers a blueprint for spiritual and physical health.

Here are three simple pledges of intent. Follow them and they can change your life.

1. I resolve to read one chapter of the Bible each day.
2. I resolve to commit to memory one passage of Scripture each week.
3. I resolve to give thanks for the energy and health that are mine.

The Bible is available to all of us. All we have to do is open it, read it, believe it, practice it.

Every careful observer knows that life ranges from mere existence at the lowest level to spiritual joy at the highest level. Some persons I have known have attained this state to a high degree of perfection. One was Dr. John Reilly. He was a member of my church, a great doctor, and a wise, understanding Christian. At one time, he professionally attended a president of the United States.

Every morning it was Dr. Reilly's habit to thank God for every organ of his body and to ask Him to bless each one that it might function perfectly. This action formula for sustained good health is a procedure well worth imitating. Here is what Dr. Reilly affirmed aloud:

Thank You, God, for my clear mind.
Thank You for my sturdy heart.
Thank You for my sound lungs, my marvelous

network of veins and arteries, my reliable
digestive system.
Thank You for my eyesight and my hearing.
Thank You for the perfection of Your creative
workmanship as it appears throughout my
body.

All his life Dr. Reilly remained healthy, alert,
and very much alive. Then one afternoon, when he
was ninety-five years of age, he lay down for a nap.
While he slept, the heavenly Father called him
home.

His nurse later told me that before he slept that
day, Dr. Reilly said, "Tell Dr. Peale that I will be
working for him from the other side." Believe me, I
am glad to have him do so, because he was a spiritual giant and medical expert on this side, and God
might indeed choose him as one of His angels of
mercy over there.

Dr. Reilly often told me that he was convinced
that our bodily health is largely determined by
what we habitually think. And he added that a
primary rule of good health is to avoid any kind of
behavior that can set up feelings of remorse or
guilt. Guilt can actually plant the seeds of sickness
in the soul, a sickness that proceeds to damage the
mind and, in time, the body. If a person has fallen
into a pattern of conduct that causes guilt feelings,
such a behavior pattern should be discarded, and
discarded quickly, if the individual wishes to remain in good health.

A woman once wrote to me, saying, "When you

come to our city, please see my husband." Formerly this man had been successful in business, active in civic groups, popular and outgoing. But then suddenly he seemed to lose vitality. He would sit and stare into space. His condition was finally diagnosed as a nervous breakdown. No one was sure of the cause, but one perceptive doctor remarked that the patient could have something weighing on his mind, which might perhaps mend if he could be persuaded to empty it out.

Eventually I saw him. His manner was dull and apathetic, and at first, he would reiterate that he "felt ill." Finally, I asked, "Is there something on your conscience that you have not told anyone? I am a pastor, and nothing you can say will shock me. So I suggest that you come clean and empty it out." I explained the effect on the body of an unhealthy mental condition. Gradually, bit by bit, out came things he had done, which he knew were wrong and sinful. When at last he had emptied out everything of this nature, he sat back, spent.

I made a heaping motion with my hands. "What are you doing?" he asked curiously.

"Heaping up all that part of your past that has weighed so heavily on your mind. Quite a mass of evil and sick stuff, isn't it? How could you expect to feel well with all that on your mind, on your soul?" I then suggested that he ask the Lord to forgive him, asserting my belief that if he did, he would get well again. He did so, then and there, praying aloud rather simply. It was a moving experience to listen to him.

Then we sat in silence for a few moments. Suddenly he stood up, raised himself on tiptoe, brought his arms over his head, took a deep breath, and exclaimed, "My, but I feel good! Oh, thank You, God, thank You, thank You!" Such was the beginning of his return to health.

It is important to remember that God not only created you, He is constantly re-creating you. The lifeforce in you is always working in a rebuilding process, causing every organ to function perfectly in harmony with God's laws. One way you can aid this process is by the use of positive affirmation. At least once every day affirm:

God's life-force is now flooding my being.
My entire body is being filled with health.
The healing grace of the Great Physician is
    sustaining me.
In Him is life; His life is in me.
I am well and strong. Praise the Lord!

Strength of body, mind, and soul is what God wants for us. He wants us to be "strengthened with all might" (Col. 1:11).

The Bible speaks of the Lord as the One who heals *all* your diseases. This is an encompassing promise. God's healing power is available for anything that may be amiss in your physical, mental, and spiritual structure. This, of course, is not to minimize in any sense the great value of medicine and surgery. On the contrary, God heals in various ways, not the least of which is through physicians, surgeons, medicines, and the instruments created by science.

Always thinking health, practicing health, affirming health will go far toward giving you good health. Dr. Paul Tournier said,

> Most illnesses do not, as is generally thought, come like a bolt out of the blue. The ground is prepared for years, through faulty diet, intemperance, overwork, and moral conflicts slowly eroding the subject's vitality. Every act of physical, psychological or moral disobedience of God is an act of wrong living, and has its inevitable consequences.

Fortunately the Lord has given antidotes against deterioration. One important method of His healing is that of joy. The Bible declares that "a merry heart does good, like a medicine" (Prov. 17:22).

Dr. John A. Schindler, a famous physician who practiced for many years in Wisconsin, wrote an important book, *How to Live 365 Days a Year*. He regularly asked his patients: "Look, are you happy and peaceful enough to live a long time?" He claimed that if he could get patients to lift their thoughts into an area of pure joy for only ten minutes every day, he could get them well, keep them well, and help them live a long life.

Robert Louis Stevenson said, "To miss the joy is to miss all." Paul Tillich, a famous scholar, said in his book *The Meaning of Joy,* "Where there is joy, there is fulfillment, and where there is fulfillment, there is joy."

A middle-aged man, whom I shall call Steve, had suffered two heart attacks. The doctors had taken good care of him in both cases, but he lived in terror of a third heart attack. He had the notion that he could survive two heart attacks, but that a third was bound to be fatal.

"Steve," I said, "you could bring a third heart attack on yourself by your fear. I get the impression that you are not happy. You exude gloom, despair, and negativism. I want to share with you what a doctor friend of mine says: 'If you are happy, you will be peaceful. And when you are peaceful, you will be happy.' Furthermore, Steve, you will be healthier as well."

Dr. Herbert Benson, quoted earlier in this chapter, says: "A positive attitude opens the vast positive possibilities of healing." Also, Dr. Benson indicates the wisdom of the Tibetan sages: "The state of your mind is the most important single factor in your physical health" (Beyond the Relaxation Response, pp. 88, 63).

The Bible is actually a book on health and well-being, and whoever practices its teachings fully and faithfully is very likely to be a healthy individual. To Steve I quoted Jesus' words found in John 14:27: "Peace I leave with you, My peace I give to you; not as the world gives do I give to you. Let not your heart be troubled, neither let it be afraid."

"Now, Steve," I continued, "When you go to bed at night and are trying to go to sleep, place your hand over your heart and imagine that it is the healing hand of Jesus. Then say, 'Let not *my* heart be troubled, neither let me be afraid.' "

Steve was deeply moved. Tears came to his eyes. So I continued, "As a pastor and a practitioner of the truths in the Bible, I suggest that every day you do as suggested. You will become joyful and peaceful. You will move into the area of pure joy. This is a powerful procedure." Steve, a sincere believer, did as I suggested. He did not have that third heart attack.

One trouble with Steve was that he had fallen into the habit of thinking too much about himself. When you put yourself in the center of all your thoughts, to the exclusion of everyone else, you are close to committing personality suicide. Self-love, self-pity, and self-interest are destructive maladies causing the personality to wither and die. A person at any age, under any circumstance, can feel better by reaching out to others. Helpful people are joyous people, and joy "does good, like medicine."

Still another mental and spiritual medicine is that of hope: "And now abide faith, hope, love" (1 Cor. 13:13). Every day send down into your mind three great words—*faith, hope,* and *love*—and your health will be stimulated.

Shakespeare said, "The miserable have no other medicine, but only hope." And he also pointed out that hope is a healing potion. Hope is indeed medicinal in its effect. When you have hope, you stand straighter, you throw back your shoulders, you breathe deeply of God's good air, and your mind is filled with healthy thoughts.

My mechanic told me my car needed overhauling. He said, "A clean engine delivers power." That is true of a human being too. Lubricate the mind with hope, and it will operate with power because with hope come aliveness, enthusiasm, vibrancy, and vitality.

Elbert Hubbard gave some priceless advice full of hope and health:

Draw the chin in, carry the crown of the head high, and fill the lungs to the utmost; drink in the sunshine; greet your friends with a smile, and put soul into every handclasp.

Do not fear being misunderstood, and do not waste a minute thinking about your enemies. Try to fix firmly in your mind what you would like to do, and then, without veering off direction, you will move straight to the goal.

Keep your mind on the great and splendid things you would like to do, and then, as the days go gliding by, you will find yourself unconsciously seizing upon the opportunities that are required for the fulfillment of your desire.

Picture in your mind the able, earnest, useful person you desire to be, and the thought you hold is hourly transforming you into that particular individual.

Thought is supreme. Preserve a right mental attitude—the attitude of courage, frankness, and good cheer. To think rightly is to create. All things come through desire and every sincere prayer is answered. We become like that on which our thoughts are fixed.

Never think of yourself as old, weary, sick, or discouraged. Never think of yourself as defeated. Hope is a form of imaging. Get hope into your mind, and change all negative thoughts into positive thoughts. Remember, there is a tendency to become what you image or visualize.

Pull yourself up, physically, mentally, spiritually, by filling your mind with hope. "Hope thou in God: for I shall yet praise him, who is the health of my countenance" (Ps. 42:11 KJV). As you hope in God, you will have health in your countenance, because you will have health of body, mind, and spirit.

A doctor had a seventeen-year-old patient who was in a coma. The boy's parents were divorced, and he had been deeply troubled before his illness. The doctor gathered the members of the broken family together, and a neighbor farmer who loved the boy was there also. The doctor sat studying his patient, then said, "All the medical signs indicate that this boy may die by morning. But actually, from a medical viewpoint, he should not die. He simply does not have the will to live. What we must do is give him a transfusion at once."

Immediately, all volunteered to give blood, but the doctor said he did not want blood. He wanted the transfusion of healthy ideas. "If we can penetrate this boy's unconsciousness, and drive faith thoughts into him, perhaps we can counteract the disease."

The farmer was a man of simple faith. He held a Bible in his big hands. He knew that Bible almost by heart, and he turned its pages lovingly. He knelt by the boy's bed, and for a long time, he read aloud passages that dealt with life, faith, love, hope, the goodness of God, and the mercy of Jesus Christ.

The family stood around the bed, each one mustering faith and transmitting it to the sick boy. Finally, as dawn was beginning to break, the boy opened his eyes, looked around, and smiled, then sank into a peaceful sleep. The doctor said, "He has passed the crisis. The 'transfusion' has been a success. The boy will live!"

In-depth faith is a profound healing power. Longer life can result from the kind and quality of the thoughts we think.

Ralph Waldo Trine, popular writer of "In Tune with the Infinite," said, "Would you remain always young, and would you carry all the joyousness and buoyancy of youth into your maturer years? Then have a care concerning one thing—how you live in your thought world." I would add that the thought most important to health and energy is the thought of God, our Creator and Re-Creator.

Repeat aloud the following health- and energy-giving affirmation:

The life-force of almighty God, my Creator and Re-Creator, is now pouring through my being, from the crown of my head, to the soles of my feet. The inflowing powerful life-force is cleansing my mind, soul, and body. It is filling me with newness of life health, and energy. For this wonderous benefit, I thank God through Jesus Christ.

May health, happiness, and God's peace be yours, now and always.

Since positive thinking is so basic in our daily living and in our search for health and energy, people sometimes ask me, "How can one be a positive thinker?" Some answers to that question are in the next chapter.

10.

How to Be a Positive Thinker

SOME PEOPLE, it seems, are just naturally positive thinkers. Others come by it the hard way.

There is, I believe, much to be said for the theory that we are all born positive thinkers. I cannot recall ever having seen a negative baby, unless perhaps one that was ill. But some, perhaps many, babies are born into negative families. Infants are highly sensitive to their atmosphere and tend to take on and absorb the prevailing mental and emotional characteristics of the family. Hence, if the family atmosphere is negatively conditioned, they become unconsciously negative in their thought processes.

They grow up to have negative mental attitudes. If later, at age twenty or thirty or so, they want to be positive thinkers, they face the problem of unlearning long-held habits of thinking, and that relearning process can take some doing. But a human being is endowed with habit-breaking power the same as habit-forming ability, and any habit can be changed. Though sometimes the cerebral grooves made by habitual thought processes run deep, they are nevertheless subject to revision if the desire to do so is sufficiently intense, the will to do so strong, and the imagination acute.

Human beings, made in the image of their Creator and possessed of His characteristics, are by nature positive because He is positive. The Creator has an astounding confidence in His creatures, for He confers upon them the right and privilege of choice. They are granted the right to choose error instead of truth, evil instead of good, wrong instead of right. They can be negative instead of positive in their thinking. But having chosen one set of values and having lived by that pattern for years, they may at any time exerise their right of choice again and choose opposite values. Christianity calls this conversion, the process by which one converts or changes the essential being. "If anyone is in Christ, he is a new creation; old things have passed away; behold, all things have become new" (2 Cor. 5:17).

So, I wish to emphasize this basic fact—you can change from negative to positive thinking and enjoy all the blessings that follow such a change. This is possible no matter how long and how completely you have been a negative-thinking person. How may I say this so confidently? I experienced this change, and if I could revamp my thinking from negative to positive, I believe sincerely that a similar change can happen to anyone who will pay the price in effort and persistence.

Since a personal experience is worth a thousand unsupported assertions, I will remind you I was badly afflicted with a horrendous feeling of self-doubt and inferiority when I was a young boy. Along with this misery was the haunting doubt about whether I could ever achieve my dreams, for I had them, or realize my goals, for I had them also. I was reared with and by people who were active mentally. But I was also surrounded, it seemed, by quite a few habitual worriers. It was always touch and go financially in our family, a situation which no doubt helped develop my sense of insecurity. Apprehension of vague but dire outcomes was in the mental atmosphere of my youth. But whatever the cause, there was added to my feelings of inferiority and inadequacy a negative attitude generally. Despite my dreams of the future, I was a negative thinker. I continued in this unhappy state until my sophomore year in college when in a miraculous way God turned around my negative pattern of looking at the world.

The number one priority in becoming a positive person is desire. You must want to be a positive person so intently that you determine to start at once the process of change in yourself. And let me assure you that if you believe you can change from negative to positive, you will do so.

There is a curious side to this changeover from negative to positive. If you are a positive person today, you may not realize just how you got to be that way. As you struggled to believe, all that time you were in the process of becoming positive. The very moment you tried, you were in the power flow of new and dynamic thought.

I was speaking along this line at a convention for the top-producing agents of a large national insurance company. An attractive, young couple, all excited, came up to me after my talk, and the man said, "I never knew before how I became a positive thinker. But in your message today you described exactly what happened to me. I just want to tell you that now I know how I achieved the success that has surprised me and that brought me to this conference as a winner. Thank the Lord," he concluded fervently, "for God did it."

He explained that he developed an intense desire to bring an end to his negative attitude which he had suffered from childhood. Though he had not been reared in a religious family, indeed quite the contrary, he nevertheless got the definite belief that only by faith in God would he ever overcome his sense of inferiority and self-doubt. He tried to hide this belief from his father who was a fanatical anti-Christian, but the older man saw through his son. "I don't believe in this God stuff, as you well know. And I've tried to rear you as an objective thinker, free of all that religious emotionalism. But, Son, if God can remove the failure-producing feeling of inferiority from you, as a fair-minded man I'll give Him the credit He deserves."

"Well, what does your father think now that you have become one of the top producers of your company and are a recognized positive thinker?" I asked.

He chuckled, "Well, Dad says if God could change

me from a defeated negative thinker to a successful positive thinker, maybe he better get acquainted with God. And he tells people, 'God did something for my own son which I was never able to do myself.' Anyway," concluded the young man, "I see clearly that what happened to free me from a deadening negativism was a spiritual process. And believe me, I'm going to stick with it."

In October of 1952 I published my book *The Power of Positive Thinking*. It was the first book ever to bear that title. It sold over fifteen million copies in forty-five languages. Since its publication, many authors have written on the same theme under various titles. But that one phrase "the power of positive thinking" has become a basic concept in the English language and culture and, by translation, in many cultures of the world.

That positive thinking works as described, I have no doubt whatsoever. A vast correspondence with readers, which began when the book was published, each letter telling how positive thinking turned a life around and lifted a person from failure to success, is evidence that millions have found new hope and new life through the principle of positive thinking. In short, it gave each person a joyous fulfillment.

To satisfy the oft-repeated demand, "I want to know more about positive thinking," I organized a Positive Thinkers Club, and every month I write a lesson on positive thinking that is mailed to every member of the Positive Thinkers Club. (For further information about the Positive Thinkers Club, write to the Foundation for Christian Living, Box FCL,

Pawling, New York 12564.) Thousands receive these lessons. Thousands of young people—teenagers and those in their twenties who were not born when my first book was written—are asking, "Tell me more about positive thinking." They want to know what it is and how they can become positive thinkers because they are convinced that this is the best of all ways of life.

Answering these questions and helping as many people as I can to live creative, happy, effective lives I take to be my mission on earth. The Lord apparently wants this mission to be fulfilled. I have been given the strength to speak constantly about positive thinking to audiences around the world, to write books on the subject, to publish *PLUS: The Magazine of Positive Thinking* ($7.00 per year—write to the Foundation for Christian Living, Box FCL, Pawling, New York 12564), and *Guideposts* magazine ($6.95 per year—write to *Guideposts,* Carmel, New York 10512), one of the phenomenal, successful publications of our time. In addition, we have two nationwide radio programs carrying the message—the Positive Thinkers Network and the American Character.

This current book was written in part to answer many questions, especially how people may become positive thinkers and continue to be positive in the ups and downs of life. So, how can you become a positive thinker and remain one?

As I have mentioned, the number one priority is desire, but even that is not enough. Intensity of desire is required. To become a positive thinker, you must want to be, not halfheartedly or wistfully, but intensely with all the wanting of which you are capable. If you do not have intensity of desire, the chances of your succeeding are minimal. But with intense desire, if it is sustained, you have the basic ingredient for becoming a positive person.

I must point out once again that some people are positive thinkers by nature, and fortunately they were never subjected as children to a prevailing negativism. For some reason, probably because of heredity or strong family influence, they proved impervious to the predominately negative attitude all around them in the world. It seems that natural positive thinkers are less numerous than negative thinkers. However, since the positive-thinking concept came upon the scene in the 1930s in the time of the Great Depression, this type of thought and action has become immensely popular. As a result, the number of persons attaining a positive attitude has greatly increased.

One night after I had spoken to a rally of several thousand sales personnel in Atlanta, a young man approached me and said, "Keep on underscoring the idea that intensity of desire is basic to gaining and maintaining a positive attitude."

He seemed so earnest about the matter that I asked, "Why, have you had experience in this connection?"

He then told me he came from a very poor rural family, that his father could never make a go of his little farm. The farm equipment, already second- or even thirdhand, was always breaking down. And since his father was constantly short of cash, hand repairs were necessary. He added, "None of us were handy. As a result of always being on the edge of poverty, conversation around home was always negative: 'We can't. We'll never get anywhere. Things are hopeless.' So ran the same old dismal outlook. I never heard any optimistic statements. Then one day some fellow spoke to our school assembly. I still don't know who he was, but vaguely I heard later that he was from the National Cash Register Company at Dayton. We lived down on the river in southeastern Ohio. He gave a talk on positive thinking, and he said if you develop the habit of thinking positively, even about the most negative conditions, you set in motion creative forces that will counteract any negative.

"This speaker was down-to-earth, had a lot of humor, was convincing, terrifically persuasive. He showed me that there could be a brighter outlook. And I wanted to be different, to get away from all that gloomy thinking and talking.

"I don't know how I ever figured it out by myself because there was no one to teach me, but I began to realize that I had to want positiveness with everything I had. I was smart enough to go to our little local library and look for a book that might help me. I found one of your books, *You Can If You Think You Can*. Then I realized the truth that what you think, if you think it hard enough, will ultimately come to you. If you think you can move up to a higher level, then with God's help you can.

"So," he concluded, "as you go around making

speeches, always remember that in every audience is someone like me who, as the Bible says, hungers and thirsts for righteousness (Matt. 5:6)."

He defined *righteousness* as "right-mindedness." This earnest young fellow had experienced both a mental and a spiritual change. He was changed in his mind and in his soul. He discovered that hungering and thirsting after something greater, call it intensity of desire, led inevitably to that which is intensely desired.

Naturally you need to know exactly what you desire so intently. Just what is positive thinking? Let me define it by describing a positive thinker. He or she is a person who is strong, tough, and rugged mentally, one who sees every difficulty but sees it straight. This person is not dismayed by any adversity, setback, or seemingly impossible condition, knowing that he or she is able with the help of the good God to see through, think through, pray through, and overcome any difficulty. To the positive thinker, there is always a way, always an answer. To every tough problem, the positive thinker says quietly, "Yeah, I know, but——!" And he may add, "The things which are impossible with men are possible with God" (Luke 18:27), or "I can do all things through Christ who strengthens me" (Phil. 4:13). Then do you know what? The positive thinker then just goes ahead and accomplishes his goals.

One thing is sure, positive thinking is not, as some negativists assert, a Pollyannish, sweetness-and-light concept. Nor is it an unrealistic, easy philosophy. On the contrary, positive thinking is for strong people: strong in faith, strong in thought, strong in character. And if they are not so when they embrace positive thinking, the struggle to become positive will make them strong.

Positive thinking is the direct opposite of negative thinking. The negativist is a disbeliever; the positive thinker is a believer. The one is full of self-doubt; the other is endowed with self-confidence. The one gives up when confronted with difficulty; the other rises to the occasion when the going gets tough. The negative thinker, by hopelessness, shuts off the flow of creative power. The positive thinker, drawing upon faith in God and self, opens wide the channels of inflowing power and creativity that produce amazing results. In short, the negative thinker tends to see, and thereby to cause, failure. The positive thinker images the possibles and attracts success to himself and his projects.

Effecting change from the negative to the positive requires, at first, beginning to entertain positive ideas about small things. Bombard your long-established negative mental attitude with small positives such as the thoughts "I can," "It's just possible," "That's going to turn out well." The mere passage of such fragmentary positive thoughts through the mind will start a fresh, though small, mental track. Repeated daily over a period of time and followed by stronger thoughts, this practice will ultimately deepen the channel forming across the mind and eventually undercut the old negative thought channel, causing it to cave in. Then the

dominant thought of your mind will be a positive
mental attitude.

One may become a positive thinker not only by
having intense desire and by retraining the thought
processes but also by learning a new manner of
speech. Speech is the audible articulation of an idea
formulated by thought in the mental process. And
repeated statements of a thought tend to imbed it
ever deeper in subconsciousness to the extent that
it eventually assumes the permanent form of a habit.
Habit is determined by constant repetition of in-
stinctive, intuitive and, sometimes deliberate, action. The ultimate of what a person becomes is a
combination of thought, speech, action, and attitude, which combination develops into habit and
finally, by reception into the deep subconscious,
solidifies one's values or point of view. This is the
process by which a person becomes either a negative or a positive thinker. It is the method by which
the mental attitude forms.

In this mind-revamping process, what you say
daily in normal conversations has a more powerful
influence on the total attitude than might be considered possible. If your usual speech is filled with
negative remarks, it indicates that your thoughts
are negatively conditioned. However, when an in-
creasing number of positive statements are spoken,
it clearly indicates that you are attempting a mental revamping, trying to shift from a negative to a
positive mental attitude. When the ear constantly
hears a positive thought which has been formulated
by the mind and spoken by the mouth, three power-

ful forces—the mind, the ear, and the mouth—are united in a campaign to change that individual from a negative to a positive thinker.

I used this idea of a combined attack on the negative habit by the mind, the ear, and the mouth in a speech to a national sales rally in Kansas City. Months later I returned to that same city to speak to the Kraft salesmen from the middle western and western states but did not include this idea in the talk that day.

On the way out of the Music Center where the meeting was held, a man intercepted me. "I barged into the Kraft meeting. I saw that you were billed to speak and figured they wouldn't mind my gate crashing. You see, I heard you when you were here some months ago when you spoke of that mind, ear, and mouth bit. Thought you might develop it further for this crowd."

Then he went on to say that he had made use of this technique because, as he put it, he was trying to work his way out of negativism. "But," he said, "I improved on your idea. I added the eye to the mind and the ear and the mouth. Then I stopped reading all the negative junk in some newspapers and magazines and books. I figured I could take in positive ideas through my eyes. So I've been reading every motivational and positive book I can find. I've got a positive-thinking library started. Anyway, I think positive, speak positive, listen positive, and see positive. Every avenue into my personality is being worked."

"And what is the result?" I asked.

"Boy, I'm so packed full of the positive that all that old negativism I went along with for years is being crowded out." He hesitated. "Hey, say a prayer for me sometime, will you?" Then suddenly he seemed to get another thought. His mind was working at full capacity. "Maybe we should add the soul to the mind, the ear, the mouth, and the eye. I'll tell you something. You just can't go with this program without the Lord going along with you." Then he shook my hand. "Got a business appointment. See you." And he was off, going strong.

Becoming a positive thinker when one has long been negative is essentially an educational process. And in that learning experience, thinking, hearing, speaking, and growing (especially spiritually) have important roles. The truth is that an individual can be what he wants to be if he knows what he wants to be and if he desires with intensity and utilizes all the forces of mind and spirit inherent within him. Then he can attain his goal of becoming a positive thinker.

It is conceivable, I suppose, that one can become and remain a positive thinker in spite of all the difficulties experienced by all men and women without emphasis on the spiritual. But I cannot imagine anyone fully overcoming negative thinking and action without the benefit of prayer and faith, without what we call spiritual experience. To overcome a profound inferiority feeling, I have personally used every method suggested in this book and in all my other ones. I must say that without spiritual help I would never have made it and been freed from negativism. The Lord saved me from myself, and if I have been able to do anything at all of a constructive nature in life, it is because He has helped me all the way. I owe everything to Him.

In the first place I finally had to admit, as a teenager, that I was never going to be able to overcome self-doubt and inferiority without help, that I simply could not do it on my own. Years later a superbenefactor of mankind named Bill Wilson, whom I had the privilege of knowing, founded a tremendous organization called Alcoholics Anonymous. Bill had tried every possible means to overcome the disease that was destroying him, but he had no success whatsoever. He told me that finally he went to the top of a high hill. There he poured out his feelings and voiced his longing for deliverance and victory. Aloud he cried out, "Help me, dear Lord, oh, please help me. I am powerless. I can do nothing on my own. Oh, please help me." He stood for a long time alone on that hilltop. But he was not alone. Presently it seemed that a strong, fresh, clean wind started blowing, and it seemed to be blowing through him, blowing him clean. All his weakness was swept away. Power flooded into him. He was re-created.

The validity of this remarkable experience is attested by the fact that Bill Wilson walked down the hill determined to bring to others the same incredible release from the destructive disease he had experienced. So it is that in every Alcoholics Anonymous headquarters, I am told, are the words, "There but for the grace of God, go I."

This particular problem was not mine. But negative thinking was and inferiority was and self-doubt was. To get over them, to be cured, I needed the same treatment Bill Wilson had, namely, a power beyond human power, the incredible power of God which is freely offered to anyone who won't quibble about it but who will humbly ask for it and receive it.

Some weaknesses fasten themselves like barnacles upon human beings. I have labeled two of them alcoholism and negativism, and both are deeply rooted in the unconsciousness. Nothing superficial will work successfully on them. They must be pulled up from the roots, their roots killed, and a profound healing method applied, a curative process that reaches to the essence of one's nature. Only the re-creative power of the Creator, almighty God Himself, can effectively deal with diseases so basic.

Therefore, if you have some intellectual notion or dilettantish idea or emotional resentment toward religion and expect to eliminate the deep roots of a negative attitude without religion, try it if you will; but I warn you that if you really want to become a positive thinker with extra power, you will have a very difficult time. I suggest that you overcome your antireligious antipathy and humbly ask God, in your own way, to help you throw off the destructive habit of a negative attitude. He likes you even if you may not like Him, and He stands ready to help anyone who asks for help.

I will never forget the irate man who walked into my New York office one bitterly cold winter afternoon and demanded to see me. "Have you an appointment?" my secretary asked politely.

"No, I have no appointment; but I need to see Dr. Peale. And get this straight ... I'm *going* to see him."

"Just a moment," she replied and came in to tell me of my "tough oddball, would-be visitor."

"Okay, bring him in," I said, aware that this man's angry actions indicated a mixed-up condition of spirit. The interview proved to be one of the most curious I ever had, and I have had many strange ones.

He seemed a well-educated, substantial man in his thirties. "Look," he said, "I would not have barged in on you if I were not in a pretty bad state, and I've just got to talk to someone. You don't know me, and I have seen you only once when you spoke to a real estate convention. Have you time to listen to me talk my trouble out?"

"Well," I replied, "it so happens that I do have scheduled appointments, but I'll give you an hour. If you organize your story, that should be sufficient time for a first interview. So go ahead."

Immediately he plunged into an angry dissertation about himself. That he was seething with self-hate was evident. His lifelong shyness and self-doubt had taken their toll. Everything was always bound to go wrong for him. He was born to lose. This was his ingrained self-image, and had he not had some inherited wealth, he would have been destitute. Of course, he was a thoroughgoing negative thinker, and he admitted being an alcoholic.

But he had a lingering hope and a flickering desire to change and become a normal person. "I know that you teach the positive-thinking idea, that you invented positive thinking. What is wrong with me anyway? What do I need?"

"Well," I replied, "it is self-evident, I think, that you need God. Only God can unravel your complicated mix-ups."

At this he became red in the face. "Is that all you can say? I expected something better of you, a well-educated man. So you're just like the rest of them. You too start talking God. God. God. God. That's all anyone can come up with. I tell you, I'm sick of all this God stuff." He jumped up and stomped angrily from the room. He did not have the politeness to thank me for my time. All I could do was send a prayer after him that in some way peace might come to this distraught fellow.

A half-hour later my secretary called on the intercom, "That man is back. I think you had better see him. He looks terrible."

I explained to the person with me that our conversation must be terminated. The man came in. He paced up and down. "Whatever has happened to me?" he asked repeatedly.

"Calm yourself, my friend, and tell me what is troubling you now."

He then explained that upon leaving my office, he walked through the streets muttering, "God. God. It's always God ... God ... God." Then he said it seemed that suddenly a bright light flashed up everywhere. Winter twilight had faded into darkness, but for him everything was brilliantly lighted. People's faces were alight, the buildings shone in white light. The usually dirty littered streets of Manhattan were clean and illuminated. People passing by seemed beautiful. He stared at them, but they gave no sign of seeing what he was witnessing. "Even the sidewalks seem to emanate light. I'm out of my mind. I'm going nuts!" he exclaimed. He did the only thing he could think of. Bewildered, he headed back to my office.

He turned a pathos-filled face upon me. "What has happened to me? Have I gone balmy?"

"No," I said, "you are in your right mind all right. Perhaps the rightest it's ever been. You have been given a rare experience, one that we call mystical. God had burst into you with power. I think you are healed. I believe you have been re-created. Don't ask me why, for I do not know why. I guess that God wants you to do something special with your life."

The outcome was that this man became a totally different person, peaceful, happy, normal, and definitely positive. In the years that followed this amazing experience, he helped many people find themselves in various ways.

In all my time of working with human problems, this man's experience was unique. The wise God's method of making positive thinkers out of negative thinkers and good people out of bad ones is usually a quieter and more evolutionary process of growth. But in whatever way He may work, one thing is sure—if you seemingly cannot make a personality change on your own, the Lord God is always there to help if you ask for that help.

Inherent in positive thinking is the positive image. The next chapter tells more about this important new ability and how you may acquire it.

11.

Happiness at Last

It is difficult to imagine anyone lower in spirit and in prospects than Ken Butterfield as he dragged himself down Second Avenue that dismal February morning. He had breakfasted frugally on toast and coffee at a joint a few blocks back, and he had exactly seven soiled one-dollar bills left in his pocket. He had spent the night in a shelter for homeless men. But he had one thing going for him, a rather decent suit of clothes, a holdover from more prosperous days. And he was fairly neat and clean.

His had been a fast spiraling comedown. His deceased father had left him about forty thousand dollars. Never having had so much, he had blown it first in posh lounges and finally in cheap bars. "I am entirely out of hope," he had told someone.

"Better see Norman Vincent Peale," that someone advised.

"Who's he, and what can he do for me?"

"Maybe give you a new idea about yourself. Anyway it might be a good idea to see him."

Thus it was that he showed up at my office that winter morning. "Tell me all about it and leave nothing out," I said.

Thus prodded, he gave me a brief life history and ended, "I'm no good at all. I'm a total flop, an absolute failure. In fact, I'm not worth a dime." So ran his complete self-depreciation.

Despite the thorough negativism of his self-evaluation, I noticed that he did not ramble or repeat but tied it all up in a neat and succinct summary. This indicated to me that he had some ability to think and express his thoughts in an organized manner.

"Smart guy," I broke in.

"What do you mean smart?"

I explained my admiration of his ability to tell his story coherently. "You've got a good mind, and anyone with a good mind can get out of any hole, however deep, providing he really wants to and is humble enough to take advice."

"No one ever told me before that I have a good mind," he grumbled.

"So what! I'm telling you now."

He took his seven dirty one-dollar bills out and laid them side by side on my desk. "That's all I have in this world," he announced solemnly.

"What do you expect me to do, cry?" I asked. "I'm not at all impressed. You've got a lot more than those seven dollars. For one thing there is that head on your shoulders we've been talking about.

Then you have youth. And if you would stand up straight, you would be a rather impressive fellow. You just told me that you have a college degree and that you graduated with honors. What do you mean that seven dollars is all you have in the world?"

I pointed out that all he had done in our conversation was to lay out his negatives. "Let's go for your assets," I said. It wasn't long before I had Ken feeling so much better about himself that he actually told me of a few ideas he had had in the past.

Unmarried, he had been assistant manager of a store before he began drinking heavily. As a result, he lost a good job, one that promised advancement. Then he really hit the toboggan. But only now was he really aware of it and ready to do something about himself. He was intelligent enough to realize that a first step was to reverse his negative thinking, drop his attitude of hopelessness and self-depreciation, and look for all the positive factors in his situation.

"Why was I so dumb as to run through that forty thousand dollars my dear father had scrimped and saved to accumulate?" he asked.

"Oh, even the smartest people do dumb things. But one of your assets is the intelligence to know when you've been dumb. You have had a very expensive lesson in how not to handle money. In the future, when you have a lot more than the inheritance you sent down the drain, you will be much wiser and more circumspect. Charge it up to education."

"Yeah, I know that makes sense, but if only I hadn't been such a dope."

"One of the greatest of all futilities is 'if only'," I said, and told him what I had learned from Dr. Smiley Blanton. Dr. Blanton said that many of his patients were emotionally ill, even physically sick, because they would not let go of the "if only I hadn't done this or had done that." Mental health is regained when the patient is able to substitute the thought of "next time" for the impotent regret of "if only." It is the "next time" concept that leads away from life's stupidities and failures and helps get creative things going again.

Despite his negative attitudes, Ken reached for positive thinking as a drowning man for a floating log. He was naturally bright, and he showed it by responding to the suggestion that a successful life-style was not at all impossible. He did not again call attention to those lonely seven one-dollar bills. But I did. It so happened that I had access to a discretionary fund, supplied to me by some generous persons for use in providing temporary help to those in need.

I said, "Ken, look, let's stop fooling around with failure. We are going to get you organized, starting now. First, I'd like you to begin the practice of affirmation. In your present condition you need a big buildup of positive thinking. So here is what you do. Use the affirmation I'm going to give you at least thirty times a day for a while. As it begins to take effect in your system, we can reduce it. But for now, take this thirty times daily. Say aloud:

1. I am in the process of creative change.
2. I am becoming better every day in every way.
3. I am firmly on the success beam.
4. My own is coming to me now.
5. God is guiding and helping me daily.

"Now, Ken," I added, "I'm going to invest a little money in you. Go to the YMCA and get a room. Go out of my office today affirming, 'There is a job for me somewhere in this big city.' Believe that. Definitely image or visualize that job. Then go out and get it and do it better than anyone ever did it before. Thank God constantly for what He is doing for you. And you are on your way."

He found the job, counterman in a small West Side restaurant. He gave the job all he had, which was plenty.

When he came to me that day, he was hopeless. He was at the bottom which, as I have pointed out, is actually a favorable spot to be since one cannot go lower than the bottom. The only direction left is upward. He reversed his thinking, canceled out the word *hopeless,* substituted for it hope and faith and positive thinking. Result? He conquered the alcoholism. He gradually moved up from counterman to manager and ended a successful, happy man.

Instead of a miserable and futile "if only," he experienced a succession of exciting "next times." The process of thinking, which brought about this happy result in the life of Ken Butterfield, can do the same in the life of Mr. or Ms. Anybody. Oh, yes,

Ken paid back every cent pronto. And those seven dirty one-dollar bills? He saved one and had it framed to hang on his office wall. His name really wasn't Ken Butterfield, but all other facts in this story are accurate. The important fact is that this man achieved happiness at last.

Two important ideas are inherent in all improvement, in all progress. One was suggested by my friend James R. Knapp when Ruth and I were having dinner with him and his wife Sally one night in Los Angeles. We were talking about how one can always do a better job and reach an improved level of personal achievement. Jim said, "It's basic to take corrective action when things are not going right." That truly lays the matter on the line. Decide to get through with what you currently are doing incorrectly. Take corrective action at once, for only then can you begin the move up to a superior performance.

Corollary to that procedure is an idea that is constantly stressed by another friend, W. Clement Stone, well-known philanthropist and publisher. "Do it now," reiterates Clem Stone. These two ideas taken together will bring about remarkable change and improvement: take corrective action and do it now.

We hear much about timing, that mystic moment when all elements are just right or the sudden awareness that corrective action is needed. Just how can a person who has been muddling along on the edge of failure or living with a feeling of inadequate fulfillment suddenly become so acutely sensitive as to know when the right time comes for taking corrective action?

In some cases a person has the power to create the correct timing. If change is to be considered, it must be right, it must be sensible, it must be within the realm of possibility. The steps are simple: stop, think, visualize, pray. If all the elements are positive, the individual can force the timing by assertive control.

I have discovered that a lot of people are doing things and doing them well, but in their hearts they would rather be doing something else. Now and then we are surprised when some very successful person suddenly changes career in midlife and becomes equally successful in a new role.

Take William Howard, for example. Again I am using a fictitious name, because this man is quite well-known. Only by promising to withhold his identity would he give me permission to tell his story. As a young boy in a small midwestern town, he was fascinated by printing shops and newspapers. He hung around the press room after school, watching compositors make up the paper, and he was thrilled by the excitement of getting the evening edition onto the streets. As a newsboy, expertly sailing his papers onto the doorsteps along his route, he dreamed big dreams of that exciting time when he would be a reporter on a big city daily or top editor of a small town paper. He got printer's ink on his fingers, and as they say, it can never be rubbed off.

But his parents had other dreams for him. They wanted him to be something else. They did not pressure him, but he well knew their desires, and so it was that he turned his back on the world of publishing to enter an entirely different line of work.

William Howard proved to be very good at it too. He became rather famous in the field of endeavor his parents wanted for him. People generally said that he was cut out for the job in which, over the years, he distinguished himself. But as he grew older and received many honors in his profession, he still dreamed of publishing. He learned that some dreams never die. At heart he was an unsatisfied publisher. Even after many years, the ink had not rubbed off.

Did what he was actually thinking make sense after all those years? Could he even contemplate leaving all he had done and actually abandon a brilliant career in one field to return to his boyhood dreams? He studied his fingers. Unlike those of the boy, they were now gnarled a bit. But the printer's ink was still there. His first love was still strong in his heart. For months he vacillated. But he had fulfilled his parents' desire, and they were long gone from this world. So why not? Then one night as he walked under the ancient maples on his farm, he made the decision. He made the turn back to boyhood dreams. He took corrective action on his career. "Do it now," something whispered. That is how he left the career of a lifetime and embarked upon a new old one. William Howard went back to publishing. And happiness came to him at last, quite like it was in boyhood's happy hour.

Every one of us is entitled, I believe, to find his or

her true self in this life. If you have run a drugstore for years but have wanted to be a musician, let's say, why not shift gears and give it a try? Or if you have been a musician but would rather run a drugstore, you are entitled to realize your dreams and be yourself. Deep inner dreams are never to be discounted in the fulfilled life. Since the Creator undoubtedly put those dreams in your heart in the first place, they have to be treated with respect. In all of this, of course, you must take your responsibilities into account.

My cousin Philip Henderson was a very successful educator. For some years he was an executive at Mount Holyoke. Later he served as president of Western College for Women at Oxford, Ohio. His father, my uncle, Hershel Henderson, was a building and loan executive, a banker and farm owner. He became a wealthy man, a leading businessman in Highland County, Ohio. He wanted Philip, his elder son, to follow in his footsteps, but the son was not made of the same stuff. He became a student, a thinker, a teacher, and in those activities he found peace and happiness as well as success. His younger brother, Howard, took over their father's business affairs and handled them very successfully. Both boys seemed to have found themselves—the one in education, the other in business.

I became a public speaker and for years have spoken almost everywhere to all sorts of public gatherings. One night Philip attended one of my speeches in a large hall in Cincinnati. Afterward in my hotel room we sat relaxing. The conversation proved memorable for me. "Norman," said Philip, "you must be pretty satisfied with yourself. You received a standing ovation from that big crowd before you spoke and another afterward. The people liked you. In fact, they thought you were great. But would you like to know what I, your cousin who has known you all your life, think about your performance tonight?" (I might say that I have an autographed picture of Philip on which he has written, "From your cousin and your best friend.")

I was prepared for a pretty forthright remark, since he has always been direct and honest. "I think," he said, "that you did not give that speech all you've got. You were coasting. All you wanted was to get it over with. Don't you really like to speak?" he asked. "I know you are completely sincere and believe what you say, but the all-out eager enthusiasm doesn't come through because somehow you don't seem to take entire joy in speaking."

His insight was accurate. I have a message of positive thinking or positive faith in which I believe with passionate fervor, but the technique of communication is always difficult. I can do it better in writing, perhaps. Speaking has always been a rather painful effort for me, and I took on a mild dislike for it which Philip picked up on.

I am very lucky to have such a good friend, someone who devotedly loves me and can, therefore, lay it out forcefully for my own good. I never forgot this conversation with my cousin who was as close as a brother. He made me see that I must love people to be effective as a speaker and I must also try to rid myself of the dislike of public speaking itself. As I have sought to achieve a more positive attitude toward public speaking, my total happiness has increased.

It is important to love what you are doing, to like your job. When you do, you are bound to give it more of yourself. And the more you give of yourself, the more life will give back to you. As someone said, "Love life and life will love you back." So, let me be your friend. If, as my cousin said, you are coasting, I urge you to release yourself more completely to give yourself, really give yourself. To the extent to which you do this, the deep happiness inherent in your nature will surge through you. After all, the important thing is to find yourself, know yourself, believe in yourself, and give yourself. Then and then only will your life become what it was meant to be, a glorious and satisfying experience every day.

As I think about the happiness I have experienced, it seems that it has come in its most acute and pleasing form when I have received a kindness or when I have given kindness. I have concluded that kindness received and kindness given are basic factors in happiness attained. Recall little acts of kindness that you have received or given, and note that they are still capable of stimulating a happy feeling even though they may have occurred long ago.

I shall never forget the morning I received word that my mother had died. I was devastated. At first I was of a mind to cancel a speaking engagement scheduled for that day on the Jersey shore. But my mother had always taught her children to carry on and fulfill their duties. Disconsolately I boarded a train. Looking out the car window and remembering life with her from the earliest years, I suddenly felt a hand on my shoulder. It was an old friend, Colonel Myron Robinson.

"Where are you going?" I asked.

"Oh, some of the boys are having a clambake down at Cape May." He was an aide to the governor of New Jersey at that time. He sat down beside me. Then seeming to detect something amiss, he asked, "What's the matter? You don't seem your usual cheery self." I told him of my mother's death. Making no response beyond placing a hand on my knee, he sat silently and, to my surprise, left the train with me at my stop. "I really don't like clambakes. So if you don't mind, I'd like to hear you speak," he explained.

Myron stayed with me all day long. When we arrived back in Penn Station, New York, he said, "I'll have to leave you here." Then he added, "You've helped me over some rough ones, son. I love you and know how you feel about your dear mother." Patting me on the back, he turned to leave, but as he did, I noticed tears in his eyes.

Myron didn't say much during that day. A long while later Myron Robinson said, "You know something? I have a happy feeling every time I think of that day we spent together." Of course he did because he gave of himself to a friend who will ever think of him as one of the kindest men he ever knew. He is gone now, but I shall never forget him. He brought peace and comfort to a friend simply by showing love. Even in sorrow, happiness began a return.

As I write this chapter, Ruth and I are in Hong Kong. Recently we were walking on a crowded high overpass, and we came to a steep flight of steps leading down to the street. Not looking too well where I was going, I suddenly stumbled and fell. Ruth was dragged down with me since she was holding my arm. We were surrounded by hundreds in the hurrying throng, and though we struggled to rise, no one came to our aid until I heard the sweet voice of a young Chinese girl saying in clear English, "Let me help you, sir." Slight though she was, she gave both of us strong assistance and then insisted upon escorting us down the precipitous flight of stairs.

We protested that we were quite all right, but she made sure of that before she would leave us. "You are very kind," I said, to which she replied, "You must know, sir, that it gives me pleasure to help." I noticed that she had a happy look on her face as she said that.

Since it appears that helping someone produces a feeling of happiness, it follows that you can increase your happiness by simply adding to the number of times you perform an act of kindness. You will discover that happiness will be your primary state of mind if you can multiply the number of kindnesses performed. A person is fortunate to make such discovery.

Quite inadvertently I participated in a small way in opening up a happier life for a stranger on the streets of New York when I took another tumble. The streets were thick with ice following a bitter cold spell. To get in my daily two- to three-mile hike, I walked this day to an office I had on lower Fifth Avenue. At one crossing on a sheet of glare ice, my feet suddenly went out from under me, and I slid on my back across the intersection, ending up prone in the gutter. I can't imagine a more helpless situation than skidding over glare ice in such a position.

Soon, bending over me was a young man wearing a parka. He hoisted me to my feet and guided me to the sidewalk. Solicitously he asked how I felt, whether there were any indications that might mean broken bones. Assured that all was well, we proceeded along the avenue together. As we came to the next street, I saw that the crossing was equally icy. The young man took my arm, and we traversed the intersection safely. "You look familiar to me," he said. "What is your name?" When I told him, he chuckled. "Wait until I tell my friends that I picked Norman Vincent Peale up out of the gutter." We parted after that cheerful banter, and I felt it was a happy episode for us both.

Very frequently happiness eludes those who are emotionally disorganized or filled with anxiety. Anxiety is a dark, mostly irrational, sometimes terrifying mental thought that something bad is going to happen. Anxiety, long-held, discolors thought processes to such an extent that happiness can scarcely develop. And so prevalent is anxiety currently that a distinguished psychiatrist has labeled it "the great modern plague."

Achieving a calm, secure mental attitude is basic to the attainment of happiness. And as you develop such a serene mental attitude, the assurance that comes from faith is most important. It is, I believe, a well-established fact that where faith is weak, anxiety will be proportionately strong; where faith is strong, anxiety will be less of a problem. As the Scripture says, "If you have faith as a mustard seed, . . . nothing will be impossible for you" (Matt. 17:20). When you know that you can handle anything that comes up, you are very likely to be a serene, happy person. Therefore, if happiness is to be yours, you must not allow anxiety to dominate you.

How can you get the kind of faith that rids you of fear, worry, and anxiety? Start thinking faith, affirming faith, and acting on the basis of faith. Practice the "as if" principle because it is very powerful. By acting as if you have faith, your consciousness will accept the idea that you do, for a fact, have faith, and you will have it. I gave this advice once to a New York business executive, and it brought him out of a breakdown and restored him to good health. He had the capacity to believe, the mental power to accept a positive idea and go with it.

This man's wife asked me to see him after his doctor told her that the illness was thought induced. The doctor believed that fear had so gripped this man that he was actually ill as a result. He was afraid, even terrorized, of a sudden heart attack. This fear was brought on by the sudden death of three rather close business associates, and it happened that all three were in the late-forty age bracket, the same relative age as himself.

Suddenly he began to picture himself as the next victim of such a devastating attack. He developed an acute anxiety neurosis. Despite medical assurance that his heart was sound and that there were no symptoms suggesting a problem, his fear produced powerfully adverse reactions.

Before seeing the patient I discussed the case with the doctor, and in our conversation I quoted the words from Job 3:25, "For the thing I greatly feared has come upon me."

The doctor nodded. "That is a true insight. A person can greatly fear something so strongly as to actually create the condition feared or bring about a similar result," he said.

"How may it be counteracted?" I asked.

He considered that question thoughtfully, then said, "Put against that scriptural statement a similar truth that what I greatly believe can also come upon me. In other words, if fear can make you sick, a strong faith can make you well. So," he concluded, "let's prescribe faith to our friend." Both of us, the doctor of medicine and the doctor of the Spirit, each in his own way, administered a healing therapy.

"I began taking huge doses of faith" is the way the man described his changed attitude. It was not easy going because fear is difficult to dislodge. But faith is more powerful than fear, and when one is determined, as he was, to get rid of the fear destroying him, he ultimately becomes a well man. He became a daily reader of the Bible, and he found one statement he credits with his healing: "I sought the LORD, and He heard me,/And delivered me from all my fears" (Ps. 34:4). "I believe that," he said, "and that did it. I found happiness at last."

Attitude has so much to do with whether we are or are not happy persons that in all my books I have stressed positive thinking. The late William Lyon Phelps, famous professor of English at Yale University, used to say that "he is the happiest who thinks the happiest thoughts." It is true that our thoughts determine whether we are miserable or happy in life. We create the world in which we live by the thought patterns that activate our minds. It follows, therefore, that if we are to achieve lasting happiness, we will have to cultivate the thoughts that produce happiness. If we permit ourselves to nurture critical thoughts, hateful thoughts, and mental attitudes other than those of goodwill and generosity of spirit, we will develop into unhappy people. We become, to a great extent, like the thoughts we habitually think.

As I said earlier, it so happens that I am writing this chapter in the city of Hong Kong where I am on a mission for *Guideposts* magazine. I remember a man I met in a hotel elevator in this city years ago. He asked, "Are you Norman Peale?" When I admitted my identity, he said he was a reader of my books and wondered if he might make an appointment to discuss a personal problem.

When I met with this man later, he told me he was the Far Eastern representative of a business headquartered in the United States. Though he had achieved a good post in his business and should be a happy person, he wasn't happy at all. On the contrary, he was "pretty disgusted." Could I make any creative suggestions? He wanted to be a positive person and get some happiness in his life.

In an effort to appraise the nature of his thoughts, I encouraged him to talk. I have found that happiness or the lack of it quite often lies in the quality of a person's thinking. It came out in conversation that he had an enormous number of dislikes of people, of groups, and of business organizations. Many of these were people he did not know personally and organizations with which he had no contact. For example, he had a strong dislike of several retail shops, whom he termed "smug stuffed shirts." I asked if he knew the managers personally, and he admitted that he did not even know their names. He had a similar feeling for the *New York Times* newspaper which he said he "wouldn't be caught dead reading." Certain people whose names appeared often in print had his antipathy, although he did not know them personally. He was a victim of strong dislikes that verged on hate, all of them irrational.

As he expressed his negative attitudes, I realized that he actually seemed to dislike himself to some extent. It occurred to me as we talked that perhaps to the next person with whom he discussed his problem, he might very well express dislike of me as well. He was pathetically mixed up, jealous, critical, totally lacking in understanding, compassion, and respect for personality.

I suggested that he take hold of his thoughts and drill himself in appreciation, in respect for all people, in seeing the best at all times. Furthermore, I urged him to change his attitude in human relations. Only then could he develop the quality of human respect that could create within his mind a spirit of happiness. He was so very unhappy that I found him ready to undertake any reasonable program. I suggested a plan for thought reversal which proved effective.

1. He was to look for the good points in the retail shops and the *New York Times* daily paper. He was to find some positive good in the organizations he hated and speak about them only when he could emphasize the positive.
2. When he found himself irrationally disliking persons, he was to deliberately invest them with the good qualities they doubtless possessed.
3. He was deliberately to send out, by thought vibrations, good concepts to cancel out the dislikes he had previously expressed so freely.
4. He was to develop the qualities of respect, compassion, and goodwill to everyone.
5. He was to believe that by a program of spiritual healing of his thoughts, he would

become a caring, generously disposed human being.

In the years following he reported now and then on his "personality rebuilding," as he called it, at which he worked in all sincerity. Most recently he wrote me, "With God's help I believe I am a different man from the one you talked with in Hong Kong and," I was pleased that he added, "I am really finding happiness at last."

Perhaps the summation is best expressed by the great German philosopher Immanuel Kant (1724–1804), "It is God's will, not merely that we should be happy, but that we should make ourselves happy."

P.S.

SOME LETTERS have a P.S. because the writer wishes to add a further word. Why not a P.S. to a book also? So here is my P.S. and a few personal words as well.

Have you wondered why I included the modifying word *Some* in the title? Positive thinking can definitely help anyone, and millions of people have creatively adapted into their lifestyle the idea of positive thinking with positive—and often dramatic—results. But some positive thinkers get more powerful results than others.

Why do these positive thinkers get results that justify calling their outcomes powerful? They get powerful results because they study and believe and practice the principles outlined with deep desire, intensity of purpose, and a persistence that sets them off from the average.

These *Some* positive thinkers have lifted themselves into an upper category of human beings called *believers.* They are a rare kind of folk who are activated by a realistic faith in their own potential. As children of God in whose image they were created, they accept positive principles as fact. They resolutely put these principles to work and thereby achieve powerful results.

Thomas A. Edison said, "If we were to do all we are capable of doing we would literally astonish ourselves." And so *Some* positive thinkers do actually astonish themselves, and they also accept as fact the promise of Jesus Christ, "If you have faith as a mustard seed ... nothing will be impossible unto you" (Matt. 17:20).

So I urge you to be a believer, an all-the-way believer in God, in life, and in yourself. I might add, the flip side of this advice is to urge you also to be a follower, a listener, a disciple under His Lordship. In so doing, you will experience life to the full and extend yourself far beyond what you may have dreamed possible. Continue to study and practice until you become one of those achieving positive thinkers who go beyond the mediocre, who surpass the average, and who, as wholehearted believers, get powerful results.

About the Author

In addition to serving as pastor of New York City's Marble Collegiate Church, Norman Vincent Peale is a prominent lecturer, radio host, and editor and co-publisher of *Guideposts* magazine. Dr. Peale, who is now eighty-eight years old, lives with his wife Ruth in Manhattan and Pawling, New York.